ADDICTION LIES

HOW TO AVOID AND DETOX YOUR ADDICTION

SHARIK AHMAD MIR

Made with ♥ on the Notion Press Platform
www.notionpress.com

Contents

About Author

SHARIK AHMAD MIR

Sharik Ahmad Mir is born in Bandipora kashmir which is known as(Alim adab & aab) . He received his degree bachelor of business administration through university of kashmir, and now currently he is pursuing his post graduation degree MBA through clusteruniversity of kashmir apart from that he wants to become an islamic scholar and civil service officer to Responsible for improvement of social infrastructure and Curbing corruption to counter poverty.

Introduction

Addiction has a high price. I have personally watched many people die because they overdosed or abused their bodies to the point of no return. This disease does not discriminate. It can, and does happen to people of all ages and all walks of life. As humans, when things get tough, we have a tendency to fall back into our old (unhealthy) patterns. In order to overcome drug or alcohol addiction – something that takes a lot of hard work and personal dedication – we desperately need support and encouragement. When we read powerful and inspiring quotes, they make sense to us. The words resonate with us internally and have a positive impact; they give us the push we need on our way to becoming our best selves.
If you're sick and tired of being sick and tired and contemplating sobriety, take a look at the five quotes below. They might just inspire you to take the first step towards the rest of your life.

"It won't be like this forever."

Addiction makes a person feel hopeless and trapped. It controls us and makes us forget who we used to be. But the path of recovery is a step towards gaining control of your life once again. You no longer have to be a slave to the disease. And with sobriety, it is possible to gain back that sense of freedom you felt you lost so long ago...

"No matter what the situation is, remind yourself "'I have a choice."

Sobriety is a choice. Ultimately, it's up to us – and us alone – to come out of denial and make the first step towards recovery. Likewise, when we're faced with an unexpected setback or a strong urge to use, we have the power to determine the outcome. Effective treatment can help us identify and overcome our triggers, as well as allow us to make our own decisions about how to respond.

"You are stronger than you think."

A lot of us think there's no way we'll ever be able to give up drugs or alcohol, but we underestimate the strength within ourselves. Sure, the easier route may be to give up and go back to our old ways, but we are fully capable of beating this disease once and for all. All it takes is focus, determination, and hard work.

"When everything seems like an uphill struggle, just think of the view from the top."

Nobody ever said getting clean was easy, and it takes discipline to maintain it long-term. And while the uphill climb may seem impossible at first, the end result is one of the most rewarding accomplishments you'll ever experience. The reward is regaining your life and reaching your true potential, making the hard work at the beginning totally worth it.

"You're worth it."

Many of us suffer from low self-esteem, which, in turn, perpetuates the cycle of addiction. But struggling with an addiction doesn't mean we're incapable, weak, or unworthy. And it certainly doesn't mean we can't change our lives around and move past the disease that has been holding us back. We are all worthy of being happy and of living our lives to the fullest. Embrace your worth as a human being and never settle for anything less than the healthy, happy, and sober life you deserve..

ONE
WHAT REALLY ADDICTION IS

Addiction is an inability to stop using a substance or engaging in a behavior even though it is causing psychological and physical harm.

The term addictionTrusted Source does not only refer to dependence on substances such as heroin or cocaine. Some addictions also involve an inability to stop partaking in activities such as gambling, eating, or working.

Addiction is a chronic condition that can also result from taking medications. In fact, the misuse of opioids — particularly illicitly made fentanyl — caused nearly 50,000 deathsTrusted Source in the United States in 2019 alone.

The American Society of Addiction Medicine defines addiction as "a treatable, chronic medical disease involving complex interactions among brain circuits, genetics, the environment, and an individual's life experiences. People with addiction use substances or engage in behaviors that become compulsive and often continue despite harmful consequences."

Many people, but not all, start using a drug or first engage in an activity voluntarily. However, addiction can take over and reduce self-control.

Addiction vs. misuse

Drug addiction and drug misuse are different.
MisuseTrusted Source refers to the misuse of a substance at high doses or in inappropriate situations that could lead to health and social problems.
However, not everybody who misuses a substance has addiction.
AddictionTrusted Source is "fact or condition of being addicted to a particular substance, thing, or activity."
For example, a person who drinks alcohol heavily on a night out may experience both the euphoric and harmful effects of the substance.
However, this does not qualify as addiction until the person experiences "chronic, relapsing disorder characterized by compulsive drug seeking, continued use despite harmful consequence, and long-lasting changes in the brain."

There is substance addiction and non-substance addiction. Some examples of non-substance addiction include:

gambling

food

internet

gaming

cell phone

sex

Someone with addiction will continue to misuse the substance or activity in spite of the harmful effects it has.

Symptoms

The primary indications of addiction are:

>declining grades or difficulty at school

>poor performance at work

>relationship difficulties, which often involve lashing out at people who identify the addiction

>an inability to stop using a substance even though it may be causing health problems or personal problems, such as issues with employment or relationships

>a noticeable lack of energy in daily activities

>profound changes in appearance, including weight loss and a noticeable abandonment of hygiene

>appearing defensive when asked about substance use

Withdrawal from substance addiction

When a person has addiction and stops taking the substance or engaging in the behavior, they may experience certain symptoms. For those who have become physically dependent on a substance, abrupt discontinuation may provoke many unpleasant symptoms, and, in some cases, it may be fatal.

When to contact a doctor

Anyone using substances, even socially, should discuss them with a doctor to ensure safe use and monitor for signs or symptoms of addiction.

However, a person with addiction may not be ready or willing to seek professional medical help, regardless of the negative impacts it is having on their health and wellness.

If a person experiences a substance overdose, those around them should seek emergency medical assistance immediately. A person who has recovered from an overdose may want to seek professional help to treat their addiction.

When a person is ready and wants help with their addiction, they may wish to contact a medical professional to discuss options for treatment. These options include rehab, therapy, detox, and medication.

Treatments

Medicinal advances and progress in diagnosis have helped the medical community develop various ways to manage and resolve addictionTrusted Source.

Some methods include:

>medication-based treatment

>behavioral therapy and counseling

>medical devices to treat withdrawal

>treating related psychological factors, such as depression

>ongoing care to reduce the risk of relapse

>Addiction treatment is highly personalized and often requires the support of the individual's community or family.

Treatment can take a long time and may be complicated. Addiction is a chronic condition with a range of psychological and physical effects. Each substance or behavior may require different management techniques.

Helpful organizations and hotlines

A person with addiction can find many organizations that may help them. A person can also call a hotline for help with their addiction.

The following organizations can be helpful for a person with addiction:

To Write Love on Her Arms: This organization is dedicated to helping people with addiction, self-harm, depression, and suicide.

Shatterproof: This organization provides educational resources and community alliances.

Faces & Voices of Recovery: This organization is dedicated to supporting and helping people with addiction, their families, and their friends.

The Amy Winehouse Foundation: This organization provides addiction support and music therapy.

A person can call the following hotlines for free assistance with and guidance for addiction:

Substance Abuse and Mental Health Services Administration
indian Addiction Centers
Crisis Text Line
National Drug Helpline
Partnership to End Addiction
National Suicide Prevention Lifeline
National Institute of Mental Health

Summary

Addiction is a serious, chronic dependence on a substance or activity. The prevalence of addiction costs the U.S. economy hundreds of billions of dollars every year.

A person with addiction is unable to stop using a substance or engaging in a behavior even though it has harmful effects on daily living.

Misuse is different from addiction. Substance misuse does not always lead to addiction, while addiction involves the regular misuse of substances or engagements in harmful behavior.

Symptoms of addiction often include declining physical health, irritation, fatigue, and an inability to stop using a substance or engaging in a behavior. Addiction can also lead to behaviors that strain relationships and inhibit daily activities.

Stopping the substance or behavior often leads to withdrawal symptoms. People should not attempt to suddenly stop using a substance or engaging in a certain behavior without medical supervision.

Addiction treatment can be difficult, but it is often effective. The best form of treatment depends on the substance and the presentation of the addiction, which varies from person to person. However, treatment usually involves medication, counseling, and community support.

TWO
WHY DO ADDICTS LIE AND MANIPULATE

Nearly every family of an addicted person encounters this shocking fact: The addicted lie and manipulate those around them. Even those who have long been close to one's heart—like one's children or a spouse—will lie to one's face, These were people who were loved and trusted, sometimes for decades before addiction came to live in the home.

It's a brutal reality that it takes some families years to come to grips with. Some families never do come to grips with it. But every day that a family fails to realize that they are being lied to and manipulated, addiction gets to thrive and maintain its of influence.

Why they do it

Why don't addicts realize that their families have their best interests at heart and want to help? Why do they lie about their drug or alcohol use and the problems it creates? Why do they make up stories about robberies or lost jobs to get money? Why do they lie about a hundred other things and manipulate families to keep them from stopping drug use or drinking?

Think of it this way: Their need for drugs is making them crazy. When cravings kick in, they are so completely overwhelmed that all other considerations—like love, truth and honor—take a back seat. The need for drugs seems as vital as breathing or having food after starving for a long period. No other thought can even co-exist in their worlds. One woman described her sensation of overwhelming need for drugs as literally making her insane.

But there's a second reason they lie and it happens as soon as the drugs take effect the very first time. It's the same reason a person can continue to use drugs after the destruction starts. Drugs immediately begin to shut down the user's ability to be analytical. As soon as the effects of the drug kick in, the user has a lowered capacity for objective thought and decisions.

So someone smoking marijuana every day can think the mellow feelings that result are desirable while quickly forgetting about educational goals that were so important just a few weeks ago. If those goals do occur to her, it's easy to make them go away with a little more weed.

A sober alcoholic can be determined to use his money wisely but after a single drink, it looks acceptable to spend all his money on booze. That analytical ability went out like a light with the first drink. In fact, this is also what happens with triggers. The effect of triggers is to lower a person's ability to be objective and so that devastating decision can be made to have a drink or use drugs again.

Morality and Ethics Soon Depart

Once those analytical, objective capacities are lowered, it's not a big jump to the loss of morals. When an addicted person is desperate to prevent withdrawal cravings and sickness, criminal acts they never ever would have engaged in begin to look like the only way they can survive. This is how a person who was honest and ethical his whole life can begin assaulting people and robbing them, breaking into houses, stealing valuables from his family or prostituting himself or herself.

Now add guilt to the mix. Guilt acts like concrete laid on top of the analytical shutdown, cravings and crimes. Now the addicted person struggles with a burden that can't be faced. The person is now locked in that destructive pattern of behavior.

Recovery—a Process of Peeling Off the Layers

For recovery to be lasting, a person must work through all these layers of damage, relieving the guilt and restoring the ability to be objective. This recovery takes time which is why there is no set time limit for the Narconon drug rehab program. Each person works his way through these layers at his own rate.

The first layer of relief on the Narconon program comes from the New Life Detoxification Program—a deep detox utilizing a sauna, moderate exercise and nutritional supplements. This combination enables the body to dislodge drug residues that remain behind even after drug or alcohol use stops. As the residues are flushed out, a person's outlook brightens and his thinking becomes clearer. Most people say their cravings are greatly reduced. Some even say cravings are gone and that their constant dreams of drug use finally stop. Now a person can begin to think for himself again.

Next, each person must learn how to face the harm that has been done and find relief from the guilt. This major step forward occurs on the Personal Values Course. Here, a person discovers how integrity was lost and learns the procedure for recovering it. Each person has the full support of Narconon staff who understand that this process is difficult to face. Those in recovery may need help working through the harm they have done to those they love. But at the end, many people feel a weight lift as they recover their self-respect and love for others.

One person completing this life skills course commented, "I feel like a weight has been lifted off my chest and I no longer have to do those things that badly affect my life. I no longer have to slowly destroy my body and my personal property."

THREE

Fourteen Rules You Must Never Break When Dealing With Addiction

When a loved one is addicted, unfortunately, one's usual patterns of thinking and behaving may not see one through to success. Dealing with a person's addiction requires a different attitude that does not come naturally to many people. Addicted persons take advantage of this to manipulate family members so they can continue drug use without interference.

The tragedy is that when the drug abuse and manipulation continue for years, the family may have no resources left with which to save the addicted person's life. It's very common for tens or even hundreds of thousands of dollars to be spent cleaning up the problems that result from addiction.

To prevent this tragedy from occurring, here are fourteen rules you must never break when someone you care about is addicted to drugs like alcohol, crack or powder cocaine, marijuana, methamphetamine, or opiates like heroin or OxyContin.

1. Don't Be Naïve

The only safe action when dealing with possible drug abuse or addiction is to eliminate naiveté entirely, no matter how much it hurts. A naive person is too willing to believe that a loved one is telling the truth, even when the evidence strongly suggests otherwise. Families get caught in this trap because the loved one was always able to be trusted before. When the effects of alcoholism, drug abuse or addiction begin to show their faces, and until a person completes a rehab program that really gets through to him, all bets are off. Being naive about alcohol or drug abuse can be—and too often is—a fatal mistake.

How to do it wrong:

A high school student's grades fall. He drops out of a number of clubs or activities. His friends change. When his parents question him, he claims that he was tired of those activities and his teachers are picking on him. He's always been so trustworthy that the family buys these stories and leave him alone till much later when the damage is much harder to repair.

How to do it right:

Parents question him about the changes. They refuse to be naive about this matter because they know that these signs commonly mean drug abuse. They talk to teachers and some of the former friends. They hear about more symptoms that might mean drug use. They escort their son to the family doctor and ask for a drug test. The positive drug test gives them real evidence that lets them know that further action is needed.

2. Don't Be an 'Enabler'

'Enablers' might believe they are helping when, in fact, they are contributing to a person's self-destruction.

As hard as it might be for some people to conceive, an enabler actually makes it possible for a person to continue to abuse drugs or alcohol. Enabling can come in an infinite number of variations. Instead of insisting a person get professional help, an enabler might let a drug-using person who is falling out the bottom live in the home, may help him find a job, lend him a car (which he uses to go get drugs), or bring food over to his house day after day.

Financing is a major way enablers allow drug abuse to continue. When the addicted person has lost all sources of income, if the family continues to support the person financially, that person can drive himself straight down a self-destructive path. It can take quite a feat of self-discipline to stop enabling because helping a person in trouble comes naturally to a loving family. A small loan, helping him find a new car after he wrecks the last one, calling around to help him find a job - all these acts of kindness may simply be prolonging the drug abuse.

How to do it wrong:

Young woman comes home and asks her parents for $500 for rent. They ask why she can't pay her rent. She says she lost her wallet and she had all her rent money in it. Although she was short on her rent the month before and she has been sick a lot lately, the parents don't ask any more questions. They get her the cash and she leaves.

How to do it right:

A young woman asks for rent money. Parents question why she can't pay rent and note that she asked for $100 to complete her rent payment just three weeks before. She makes the claim about the lost wallet. Instead of enabling, dad says the loan depends on his being able to see her records of recent expenses and paycheck stubs. They can log into her bank account or run over to her apartment and get the records. She can't support her lies and the family does not enable her drug abuse by giving her money that will just go directly to her dealer. They can now work on her real problem.

3. Reject the Lies and Manipulation

When there are signs of being addicted, expect the lies and manipulation to occur, and you will not be caught off-guard when they do.

When a person becomes addicted, it's almost as though there is a special skill set that goes along with it. The mind becomes the servant of the drugs. He becomes expert at lying his way out of tough situations. He also learns how to turn the tables on someone trying to save his life, making it their fault that he is abusing drugs.

Grasp these two facts:

1.Along with drug abuse comes a moral and ethical decay.

2.Cravings for more drugs or alcohol can be so overwhelming that the user feels crazy. He feels totally justified in saying or doing anything necessary to get people to leave him alone so he can continue to abuse drugs. It feels as essential as breathing for him to do this.

So you don't need to be surprised when the lies come. You will need to sharpen your detective skills, verify the stories, and refuse to let yourself be manipulated. You don't deserve it.

How to do it wrong:

A wife notes that her husband is not leaving for work and has a new dent in his truck. She asks what happened. The husband replies that at work, a delivery truck backed into him and when he asked for compensation, he got fired. He was tired of that job anyway and he's going to take some time off from working. The wife notes that because there seems to be money missing out of the budget each month, many bills are already past due. She objects to his taking time off when there are bills that need to be paid. Her husband turns on her, accusing her of not being supportive of his need for some time off. After all, she took two years off after the babies were born. He berates her and belittles her until she yields and tells him to do whatever he wants to do.

How to do it right:

This example presents a difficult situation that simply may require outside help. The support of other family members, family doctor or minister or an interventionist may be required to fully cut off the husband's attempts at intimidation or manipulation. Addiction is a powerful and clever enemy. A helpless spouse, a middle-aged divorced mother, or ailing father, or worst of all perhaps, an elderly grandmother may not have the ability to hold up against this kind of direct assault. The person being lied to or manipulated needs to start by realizing that she is not the one creating this situation. She needs to find sufficient support to deal with it.

In this example, the wife hears the lies and doesn't reply. She notes all the recent upsets, illnesses and money missing and comes to her own conclusion. She recruits the assistance of other strong, trustworthy family members. The employer is consulted and it turns out the husband was fired for dealing drugs on the work premises. Soon, the addicted person is faced by a group that demands a drug test and then rehab if the drug test is positive.

4. Follow the Money

This rule is as true when it comes to drug addiction as it is with as many other types of shady dealings.

The supply of drugs and alcohol is completely fueled by money. When a person becomes a heavy drinker or drug user, there are going to be financial effects. Money is going to be missing. As addiction increases, this could be lots of money, even thousands of dollars a week.

Addicts very commonly become unable to maintain steady employment, meaning that the supply of money will dry up. When income dries up, a drinker or drug user will first sell off personal valuables and then will usually steal from family and friends. Many become desperate enough to turn to crime to pay for the drug habit. Shoplifting, identity theft, car theft, pharmacy robberies, muggings, prostitution and of course drug dealing keep the habit financed.

If you see dramatic, unexplained changes in financial conditions—either disappearing money or too much money or new, valuable possessions on hand—consider the possibility of drug addiction and related crime.

How to do it wrong:

A young man is away at college and calls frequently for more money. The family questions him about why he needs so much more money but he always has a story ready, always something different. Books prices are higher, his car needed a big repair or his rent went up. It seems like there is $1000 more needed every month. Since his stories always sound plausible, the family just sends more money, figuring they must have planned wrong when they sent him to college.

How to do it right:

Three months in a row, the young man calls for more money, always with a plausible story. The third month, they send part of the money asked for then plan a fast trip to the college campus to see for themselves. On arrival, they can see that their son has lost weight and has sores on his face. Their money has been going to heroin. They can now address the heroin addiction.

5. Protect Your Valuables

When signs of drug use and addiction start showing up, don't be afraid to secure your valuables. A person who has given up control of his life to drugs, unfortunately, loses his good judgment as well. While there are exceptions, most heavy drug users will become desperate enough to steal and rob when it looks like there are no other alternatives. If he has keys to your home, you may notice valuables like televisions, computers or tools missing. He may come in at night and take cash from a purse or wallet. It's not uncommon to hear of jewelry and even heirlooms being pawned off. One father sold all the children's toys out from under the Christmas tree. Valuables are not safe in the hands of a person struggling with addiction.

You should not feel guilty about protecting what is yours. Store valuable items elsewhere or get a safe. Install an alarm, security doors or video surveillance. Change locks both at home and at any business locations. Change security codes, passwords and signature cards. Cancel credit or debit cards you have handed over to the drug user. Discuss protecting accounts with your banker.

This should not be a last resort when you are dealing with addiction, it should happen the moment you realize there is a problem. By protecting your property, you actually enable yourself to provide the right kind of help—effective rehab—when it is needed. An addicted family member can bankrupt a family before they have a chance to get him into treatment.

How to do it wrong:

A woman is the manager of the family-owned restaurant. She begins using cocaine at the restaurant with a couple of the employees. Soon, the profitability of the restaurant falls off. Before long, it is not even breaking even. Her parents, the founders of the restaurant, try to find out what is happening. She claims employees are stealing things and fires a couple of people (the ones who do not use cocaine). The losses continue after the firings and she continues to offer excuses. The parents finally arrive at the restaurant, look at the books and realize they are bankrupt. The daughter takes off with the remaining cash. The parents do not have the money to find her and pay for her rehab.

How to do it right:

The family realizes the restaurant is losing profitability. The daughter provides excuses. The father heads to the restaurant and talks to the employees. A long-time employee finally tells him that the daughter has been using cocaine at the restaurant. "She said you knew and didn't care," he adds. Dad immediately secures all accounts, changes the locks on the restaurant, changes signature cards. The losses add up to thousands of dollars but hundreds of thousands and the value of the restaurant are saved, meaning the family can afford rehab to save their daughter's life.

6. When There are Mysterious Problems That Just Won't Resolve No Matter What, Consider Substance Abuse

When a person is using drugs or drinking excessively, it is not unusual for him to hide his habits. A teenaged boy may escape at night to smoke weed or drink with his friends—or worse. He and his friends may raid family medicine chests and pool their prescription drugs. An alcoholic wife may drink while her husband is at work and do her best to hide the evidence. The drive to abuse these drugs is so strong that addicts learn how to keep others from interfering with their habits.

But substance abuse routinely leads to problems in life, such as: Illnesses and financial problems. Arrests for DUI, possession of drugs or crimes committed to get the money for drugs. Domestic or child abuse or neglect. Loss of jobs; missing possessions that were sold for drugs. Even homelessness. A family who is trying to help a loved one through problems like these may wonder why all their efforts seem ineffective. Every time they lend him money or help him find a job or get out of jail, more problems come up. In this situation, a family should consider that the root of all these problems could be substance abuse.

How to do it wrong:

A married couple is facing severe financial problems and is preparing to file for bankruptcy. The wife can't get the husband to contribute any help toward resolving the financial problem despite repeated attempts. Right in the middle of this problem, he walks out on his job and starts disappearing for days at time. He starts having mysterious physical problems and losing weight. The wife can't understand the change in his behavior from earlier days when he was reliable. She never considers that he might be abusing drugs when he is away from home.

How to do it right:

When her husband's behavior becomes erratic and completely different from his earlier pattern, the wife realizes that something serious is interfering with his abilities. She brings in his family for help and together, they manage to track him down and find him abusing methamphetamine during those times he disappears. His addiction to this drug explains the current financial disaster and his health problems. With the correct reason for the problems, the family can seek the correct solution.

7. *Keep the Responsibility Where It Belongs*

An addicted person will make every attempt to shift the blame to others—it's just the nature of addiction.
One of the more frustrating aspects of addiction is the addicted person's immediate effort to blame someone else for his problems. Lost jobs, broken marriages, arrests, illness, bankruptcy, injury, addiction itself—they are all someone else's fault. Don't get caught believing a steady stream of stories about how other people have caused the person's problems.
On the other hand, appealing to the person's better judgment will seldom work. That judgment is buried under months, years or decades of self-destruction and harm to others that he now cannot face. Drug and alcohol abuse lower awareness. Bringing a person back to responsibility must involve a process of gradual unburdening so as to not overwhelm a person to the point of relapse. This is the job of a good rehab program.
But for the moment, do not accept that everyone else is the cause of the addict's problems. As soon as this pattern emerges, discover the facts for yourself. If it's not possible, at least insist on not being sucked into the misleading tactics of the addict. There are injustices in life, but in the vast majority of cases, a person creates or at least majorly contributes to his own situation in life. And even when life hands one a low blow, it is one's responsibility to buck up and handle it. One thing to look for is any effort on the addict's part to overcome his or her problems in a responsible manner. If this effort is absent, the likelihood increases that the full truth is being concealed.

How to do it wrong:

A father comes home after losing a job. This occurs after several months of worsening mood and relations at home. His wife sees that he spends no time with her or the children anymore and there are increasing arguments. He loudly explains how the boss is a jerk and got things all wrong and he got fired as a result. He even makes a few vaguely threatening comments about "getting back at his boss." The wife could make one of two mistakes at this point - either believe the whole tale and sympathize, or appeal to the better judgment of the husband and try to get him to see how he could have avoided being fired, "for the sake of the children." The former approach is going to let the husband live a lie and will enable matters to continue to go downhill. The latter approach, no matter how accurate, could lead to a violent argument.

How to do it right:

The best choice here is likely to be one very similar to that presented in, "Reject the lies and manipulation" rule: Enlist the support of the extended family to get to the bottom of the problem. Especially when there are children involved, don't try to deal with a stronger, more threatening person on your own. Also, don't let your shyness or embarrassment stand in the way of asking for help. If the first person you ask won't help you, keep asking until you get help. When someone is struggling with addiction, it is not unusual for it to require the efforts of a group for the problem to get fully handled.

8. Head Off Drug Abuse Before the Teenaged Years

In this modern world, expect drug influences to start very young. Parents may wait until children are in their teens to start talking about drugs but many children will already have begun substance abuse by this time.

It is tragic that this rule even needs to be written. But in today's world, waiting until the teenaged years to talk about drugs is far too late. By this age, if a youth has not started abusing drugs or drinking, he has probably seen people stoned, drunk or high and has watched drug abuse at school, parties, at home. He has seen drug and alcohol abuse in movies and on television and has heard about his sports or music heroes going to rehab. Drugs are unfortunately part of young children's lives and this was probably not as true for today's parents when they were the same age.

Most parents do not feel fully prepared to cover the subject thoroughly with their children. They may need to educate themselves on the types of drugs the children are being exposed to. There are many new drugs on the market and many youth also abuse prescription drugs or a combination of prescription drugs. Drinking is common among high school students as well.

How to do it wrong:

Gather your children up and announce that you expect them not to use any drugs. Talk about alcohol and marijuana only. Warn them that they will be grounded for an extended period if they are found to be using any drugs and leave it at that.

How to do it right:

Do your homework. Learn what drugs today's youth are being offered or seeing other people use. You can find detailed reports on their exposure in the annual Monitoring the Future report (http://www.monitoringthefuture.org/).

To learn more about the drugs they are being offered, using or seeing others use, visit the drug education resources on the Narconon International website:Drug information.

Narconon drug education classes start as early as first and second grade. It is recommended that you begin to proof your children against drug abuse at this very early age. Of course you will have to scale your message to the age of the children you are talking to, keeping things very simple and basic in the early lessons. In an age-appropriate manner, start talking to your children individually or together, as you feel would work best with their personalities. Let them know that you will help them understand the dangers involved in alcohol, nicotine, and other drugs and this will be done in short meetings held over a period of time. In each meeting, provide a short lesson on the harm that can be done by alcohol and/or other drugs. Gradually educate your children on the different drugs they will hear about and why each one is dangerous. Explain what you have learned about why people start using alcohol and drugs. Encourage them to ask questions, and if you think your children are old enough, ask them if they have ever seen anyone using that drug. Refrain from criticizing them for their observations. Try to make this a safe time to bring up things they are curious about.

9. When Choosing a Rehab Program, Do your Own Homework

There are all kinds of rehab programs available. Short-term and long-term, inpatient and outpatient. Ones that employ substitute drugs and ones that utilize nutritional supplements, yoga, massage or exercise. Wilderness programs and boot camps. Ones that are close by and ones that are far away. Programs employing animals, music or theatre in therapy and ones that teach problem-solving skills in a classroom.

It will take a little education to sort out these different types of programs. When a loved one is addicted to drugs or alcohol, every day could bring a new problem, arrest or health crisis. But a short time spent making sure that the rehab you choose is the best one for your situation may pay off with a much better result. This could mean that you avoid repeated trips to rehab.

How to do it wrong:

A family finally gets the agreement of an addicted loved one to go to rehab. Because they have not looked at the different types of programs that are available, they choose one that is right around the corner. It's a short-term program with no after-care plan. Because of the complex nature of addiction, their loved one does not have enough time or service to unravel all the addictive behavior he has learned from his years as an addict. And his drug-using friends stop by to see him in rehab, meaning that he never really gets away from the influences that helped keep him addicted. He only has 28 days of clean and sober time as a result of this program and goes back to abusing drugs as soon as he is discharged.

How to do it right:

The family researches the different types of rehab, even asking a local librarian to help them find information since they are not very familiar with using the internet. They decide on a program that is hundreds of miles from home so that the person is not continually faced with the people and places associated with drug use. They choose a longer-term program after asking the center for phone numbers of parents of other people who have gone through that program. Encouraged by comments from these parents, they have confidence that this program will enable their loved one to discover why he was using drugs in the first place and recover from his addictive habits.

10. Once the Person is in Rehab, Don't Believe Everything You Hear

When you get calls from the person in rehab, listen to them when they talk about the rehabilitation facility but take their initial complaints with a grain of salt. Drugs are a powerful master and exert an overwhelming level of control over people, especially after they first arrive in rehab. The drive to get out of rehab and get more drugs will overpower many people's desire to get sober. This is why some people try to smuggle drugs into a rehab or why they will find "vital" reasons why they "must" go home for a few days.

It's unfortunate that some people in recovery are so driven to return to drug abuse that they will invent stories of upset, harm or danger, just to get families to come get them. Of course, you must pay attention to what they say, just in case there is some mismanagement at a facility. It is wise to build a personal relationship with someone in the center you feel you can have confidence in, just for this situation.

If you have done your homework in the beginning, you have chosen a facility you have confidence in and perhaps you have even talked to other parents of graduates from that program. When you are using your judgment in this matter, realize that the real enemy is drugs, and it may be the urge to use drugs again that is motivating the upsetting call you are having to deal with.

How to do it wrong:

After many years of her heavy opiate abuse, a father sent his daughter to a rehab. Early in the program, before she found any relief from the cravings, she called her father repeatedly, crying, manipulating him, and asking him how could he send her away if he loved her? He relented and let her come home. The daughter immediately returned to opiate abuse.

How to do it right:

When the daughter called home from the rehab and tried to manipulate her father's emotions, the father was too sure of his choice of rehab to fall for her lies. He knew that the rehab had a good record of helping people recover so he decided he had to stick with his original decision. If he felt like wavering, he talked to the person at the facility he felt the most comfortable with and found out that his daughter was being a source of problems at the facility, but was actually just starting to respond to the steps of the program. A few months later, she completed the program that enabled her to stay sober for the long term.

11. Continue to Provide Support Once Your Loved One Completes Rehab

Once a person graduates from a thorough rehabilitation program, don't act like the problem never existed. Nearly everyone who completes rehab and returns home will need a period of support from family and friends. Supporters should be sensitive to the person's needs and either not drink in front of him or carefully ensure that it is not a problem. The recovered person should not be invited to drink, in fact, it would be wise for someone close to the recovered addict to serve as a backup, to take the person aside if it looks like they are going to give in and order a drink or begin to indulge in some other fashion. It should go without saying that family and friends should not abuse prescription drugs or use illicit drugs in their vicinity. While the amount of support needed will vary from person to person, it is much safer to assume that support is needed. Do not rely on or expect pre-addiction patterns of thinking and behavior until a proven, effective rehab program has been completed and a person has had enough time to assume control of his sober life.

How to do it wrong:

When an adult son comes home from rehab, mom and dad throw a party to celebrate. Because his drug of choice was opiates, they feel okay about serving beer at the party. He has a few beers. His old buddies are there (his family didn't know that they were his drug-using companions) along with an ex-girlfriend. The family then returns to their usual schedules and patterns of living, but the adult son goes out the next day and finds his old drug dealer.

How to do it right:

When the son comes home, mom and dad sit down with him and find out what he's ready to face and what he needs more time to prepare for. He realizes he has to step back into a normal life gradually. He's got a job ready and just wants to go from work to home for a while, maybe go a few places with the family. He does not want to face old drug-using associates quite yet. After he builds up a history of sober living in his home environment, he feels a little more confident about venturing out alone. When the parents leave for the weekend, another family member stops by to check on how he's doing. Within a couple of months, he's comfortable about resuming a normal pattern of living.

12. *Realize That Life Will Offer a Recovering Addict Serious Triggers to Relapse, No Matter How Good Rehab Was*

Relationship breakups, professional setbacks, job losses, lawsuits, deaths of family or close friends—these can be overwhelming. Even a person who has been sober for many years may break at these moments. When you love someone who has recovered from addiction, if he encounters one of these serious stressors, give him or her extra help at this time. Try not to leave him alone for the first few days. Once the crisis is past, the person's skills and training will be more likely to carry him through any steps that must be taken.

How to do it wrong:

A man successfully completes rehab and spends many years sober, managing a successful life. When he's out with close friends, one of them dies suddenly of a heart attack, right in front of him. Because he has been sober for a decade, the family never thinks that he would need extra support at this time. But the loss is so shocking and overwhelming that even ten years of sobriety is not enough to prevent him from relapsing into drug use. His brief escape into opiates is enough to trigger the whole pattern of addiction for him. A few weeks later, the family realizes they have lost him to addiction again.

How to do it right;

When the man's close friend dies in front of him, his brother realizes that this event could be so overwhelming that it could drive him to escape the pain with opiate abuse. He immediately goes to his brother's side and stays there for the next few days. If he has to leave, he makes sure he is replaced with another sober family member or close friend until the crisis is over. The man's brother realizes that this inconvenience to his life is nothing compared to the disruption that would occur if the man had to go through an entire rehab program again.

13. Don't Lose Hope of Recovery

If rehab didn't work once, it doesn't mean that it never will. Forty-nine years of experience helping the addicted find responsible sobriety at Narconon drug rehab centers have proven that the overwhelming majority of people will respond to caring help and a proven rehab program. Only a very few will prevent themselves from ever being helped.

If completion of one rehab program does not result in lasting sobriety, you don't have to lose hope. Your loved one may simply need more help or may need a different type of program with a different approach to repairing the damage from addiction. Your faith in the person's recovery can be the factor that saves his or her life.

How to do it wrong:

A young woman spent many years addicted to opiates and going through one rehab program after another. After several times through the same kind of short-term program, her family gave up on finding another rehab for her. They felt they had no choice but to just turn their backs on her.

How to do it right:

Despite her half-dozen trips to rehab, the young woman's father refused to give up on her. For her seventh trip, he looked for and found a completely different type of rehab, a longer-term one that would give her all the time she needed to recover from her addiction. At her graduation from this program, she told her family how much she appreciated the chance to do a program that really gave her the life skills and help she needed to get sober and expressed her gratitude to her father for not giving up on her.

By finding the right rehabilitation, you can have the person back in your life to love and laugh with again.

14. *Realize You Are Not Alone*

Many families feel totally isolated when someone in the family is addicted. They may be ashamed of having a problem like this. Many families don't reach out for help and advice because of this shame.

Wives may feel that asking for help from other family members will make them look bad in some way or maybe they would feel terribly embarrassed. Parents may even feel that the addiction of a son or daughter is somehow their fault when they actually had little or nothing to do with it at all.

The truth is that more than two million Americans enter drug or alcohol rehabs each year. Many of today's drugs are so addictive that just a few experimentations with a drug like crack cocaine, ecstasy, or prescription opiates can hook a person. Addiction is a broad social problem, and family failure may not play any significant role in the person's drug abuse.

The most important thing is that the addicted person gets the right kind of help. Feelings of shame, failure or embarrassment need to be put on the back burner until the right rehab program is found and the person is safely on his way to sobriety.

How to do it wrong:

A wife is being constantly criticized and belittled by her alcoholic husband, even slapped around. The children are terrified of their father and are often sick. The wife is too embarrassed to admit the problem or find any help from her minister, her family or her doctor. She has been convinced by her alcoholic husband that all the problems are her fault. And so the problem can continue, month after month.

How to do it right:

After some months of abuse by the husband with the worsening alcohol problem, the wife sees that she and the children are getting sicker and more depressed day by day. After careful review of her options, she admits the problem to close family members and asks for help. The family supports her by protecting her and the children while insisting that the husband enter an alcohol rehab program. The family is reunited after he recovers his sobriety.

Message for Families from Narconon

Addiction is one of life's most difficult situations to deal with. A family member struggling with this problem should realize that his or her struggle is normal. Dealing with addiction is never easy. By using the guidelines above while the problem exists, families can prevent far worse problems and losses and can arrive at a solution faster.

In over five decades of working with addicts to fully recover, Narconon staff around the world have seen that families suffer right along with the addicts. This advice is offered to help during this critical time. For more information or help, contact us or call us to speak with a consultant.

FOUR

SUBSTANCE USE DISORDER (DRUG ADDICTION)

Drug addiction, also called substance use disorder, is a disease that affects a person's brain and behavior and leads to an inability to control the use of a legal or illegal drug or medicine. Substances such as alcohol, marijuana and nicotine also are considered drugs. When you're addicted, you may continue using the drug despite the harm it causes.

Drug addiction can start with experimental use of a recreational drug in social situations, and, for some people, the drug use becomes more frequent. For others, particularly with opioids, drug addiction begins when they take prescribed medicines or receive them from others who have prescriptions.

The risk of addiction and how fast you become addicted varies by drug. Some drugs, such as opioid painkillers, have a higher risk and cause addiction more quickly than others.

As time passes, you may need larger doses of the drug to get high. Soon you may need the drug just to feel good. As your drug use increases, you may find that it's increasingly difficult to go without the drug. Attempts to stop drug use may cause intense cravings and make you feel physically ill. These are called withdrawal symptoms. Help from your health care provider, family, friends, support groups or an organized treatment program can help you overcome your drug addiction and stay drug-free.

Syptomms

>Drug addiction symptoms or behaviors include, among others:

>Feeling that you have to use the drug regularly — daily or even several times a day

>Having intense urges for the drug that block out any other thoughts

>Over time, needing more of the drug to get the same effect

>Taking larger amounts of the drug over a longer period of time than you intended

>Making certain that you maintain a supply of the drug

>Spending money on the drug, even though you can't afford it

>Not meeting obligations and work responsibilities, or cutting back on social or recreational activities because of drug use

>Continuing to use the drug, even though you know it's causing problems in your life or causing you physical or psychological harm

>Doing things to get the drug that you normally wouldn't do, such as stealing

>Driving or doing other risky activities when you're under the influence of the drug

>Spending a good deal of time getting the drug, using the drug or recovering from the effects of the drug

>Failing in your attempts to stop using the drug

>Experiencing withdrawal symptoms when you attempt to stop taking the drug

Recognizing unhealthy drug use in family members

Sometimes it's difficult to distinguish normal teenage moodiness or anxiety from signs of drug use. Possible signs that your teenager or other family member is using drugs include:

1.Problems at school or work — frequently missing school or work, a sudden disinterest in school activities or work, or a drop in grades or work performance

2.Physical health issues — lack of energy and motivation, weight loss or gain, or red eyes

3.Neglected appearance — lack of interest in clothing, grooming or looks

4.Changes in behavior — major efforts to bar family members from entering the teenager's room or being secretive about going out with friends; or drastic changes in behavior and in relationships with family and friends

5.Money issues — sudden requests for money without a reasonable explanation; or your discovery that money is missing or has been stolen or that items have disappeared from your home, indicating maybe they're being sold to support drug use

Recognizing signs of drug use or intoxication

Signs and symptoms of drug use or intoxication may vary, depending on the type of drug. Below you'll find several examples.

Marijuana, hashish and other cannabis-containing substances

People use cannabis by smoking, eating or inhaling a vaporized form of the drug. Cannabis often precedes or is used along with other substances, such as alcohol or illegal drugs, and is often the first drug tried.

Signs and symptoms of recent use can include:

1.A sense of euphoria or feeling "high"
2.A heightened sense of visual, auditory and taste perception
3.Increased blood pressure and heart rate

4.Red eyes
5..Dry mouth
6..Decreased coordination
7.Difficulty concentrating or remembering
8.Slowed reaction time
9.Anxiety or paranoid thinking
10.Cannabis odor on clothes or yellow fingertips
11.Major cravings for certain foods at unusual times

Long-term use is often associated with:

1.Decreased mental sharpness
2.Poor performance at school or at work
3.Ongoing cough and frequent lung infections

K2, Spice and bath salts

Two groups of synthetic drugs — synthetic cannabinoids and substituted or synthetic cathinones — are illegal in most states. The effects of these drugs can be dangerous and unpredictable, as there is no quality control and some ingredients may not be known.

Synthetic cannabinoids, also called K2 or Spice, are sprayed on dried herbs and then smoked, but can be prepared as an herbal tea. A liquid form can be vaporized in electronic cigarettes. Despite manufacturer claims, these are chemical compounds rather than "natural" or harmless products. These drugs can produce a "high" similar to marijuana and have become a popular but dangerous alternative.

Signs and symptoms of recent use can include:

A sense of euphoria or feeling "high"

Elevated mood

An altered sense of visual, auditory and taste perception

Extreme anxiety or agitation

Paranoia

Hallucinations

Increased heart rate and blood pressure or heart attack
Vomiting
Confusion
Violent behavior

Substituted cathinones, also called "bath salts," are mind-altering (psychoactive) substances similar to amphetamines such as ecstasy (MDMA) and cocaine. Packages are often labeled as other products to avoid detection.

Despite the name, these are not bath products such as Epsom salts. Substituted cathinones can be eaten, snorted, inhaled or injected and are highly addictive. These drugs can cause severe intoxication, which results in dangerous health effects or even death.

Signs and symptoms of recent use can include:

Feeling "high"
Increased sociability
Increased energy and agitation
Increased sex drive
Increased heart rate and blood pressure
Problems thinking clearly
Loss of muscle control
Paranoia
Panic attacks
Hallucinations
Delirium
Psychotic and violent behavior

Barbiturates, benzodiazepines and hypnotics

Barbiturates, benzodiazepines and hypnotics are prescription central nervous system depressants. They're often used and misused in search for a sense of relaxation or a desire to "switch off" or forget stress-related thoughts or feelings.

Barbiturates. An example is phenobarbital.

Benzodiazepines. Examples include sedatives, such as diazepam (Valium), alprazolam (Xanax), lorazepam (Ativan), clonazepam (Klonopin) and chlordiazepoxide (Librium).

Hypnotics. Examples include prescription sleeping medicines such as zolpidem (Ambien) and zaleplon (Sonata).

Signs and symptoms of recent use can include:

Drowsiness
Slurred speech
Lack of coordination
Irritability or changes in mood
Problems concentrating or thinking clearly
Memory problems
Involuntary eye movements
Lack of inhibition
Slowed breathing and reduced blood pressure
Falls or accidents
Dizziness

Meth, cocaine and other stimulants

Stimulants include amphetamines, meth (methamphetamine), cocaine, methylphenidate (Ritalin, Concerta, others) and amphetamine-dextroamphetamine (Adderall XR, Mydayis). They're often used and misused in search of a "high," or to boost energy, to improve performance at work or school, or to lose weight or control appetite.

Signs and symptoms of recent use can include:

Feeling of happy excitement and too much confidence
Increased alertness
Increased energy and restlessness

Behavior changes or aggression
Rapid or rambling speech
Larger than usual pupils, the black circles in the middle of the eyes
Confusion, delusions and hallucinations
Irritability, anxiety or paranoia
Changes in heart rate, blood pressure and body temperature
Nausea or vomiting with weight loss
Poor judgment
Nasal congestion and damage to the mucous membrane of the nose (if snorting drugs)
Mouth sores, gum disease and tooth decay from smoking drugs ("meth mouth")
Insomnia
Depression as the drug wears off

Club drugs

Club drugs are commonly used at clubs, concerts and parties. Examples include methylenedioxymethamphetamine, also called MDMA, ecstasy or molly, and gamma-hydroxybutyric acid, known as GHB. Other examples include ketamine and flunitrazepam or Rohypnol — a brand used outside the U.S. — also called roofie. These drugs are not all in the same category, but they share some similar effects and dangers, including long-term harmful effects.
Because GHB and flunitrazepam can cause sedation, muscle relaxation, confusion and memory loss, the potential for sexual misconduct or sexual assault is associated with the use of these drugs.

Signs and symptoms of use of club drugs can include:

Hallucinations
Paranoia

Larger than usual pupils
Chills and sweating
Involuntary shaking (tremors)
Behavior changes
Muscle cramping and teeth clenching
Muscle relaxation, poor coordination or problems moving
Reduced inhibitions
Heightened or altered sense of sight, sound and taste
Poor judgment
Memory problems or loss of memory
Reduced consciousness
Increased or decreased heart rate and blood pressure

Hallucinogens

Use of hallucinogens can produce different signs and symptoms, depending on the drug. The most common hallucinogens are lysergic acid diethylamide (LSD) and phencyclidine (PCP).

LSD use may cause:

Hallucinations
Greatly reduced perception of reality, for example, interpreting input from one of your senses as another, such as hearing colors
Impulsive behavior
Rapid shifts in emotions
Permanent mental changes in perception
Rapid heart rate and high blood pressure
Tremors
Flashbacks, a reexperience of the hallucinations — even years later

PCP use may cause:

A feeling of being separated from your body and surroundings
Hallucinations
Problems with coordination and movement
Aggressive, possibly violent behavior
Involuntary eye movements
Lack of pain sensation
Increase in blood pressure and heart rate
Problems with thinking and memory
Problems speaking
Poor judgment
Intolerance to loud noise
Sometimes seizures or coma

Inhalants

Signs and symptoms of inhalant use vary, depending on the substance. Some commonly inhaled substances include glue, paint thinners, correction fluid, felt tip marker fluid, gasoline, cleaning fluids and household aerosol products. Due to the toxic nature of these substances, users may develop brain damage or sudden death.

Signs and symptoms of use can include:

Possessing an inhalant substance without a reasonable explanation
Brief happy excitement
Behaving as if drunk
Reduced ability to keep impulses under control
Aggressive behavior or eagerness to fight
Dizziness
Nausea or vomiting
Involuntary eye movements
Appearing under the influence of drugs, with slurred speech, slow movements and poor coordination
Irregular heartbeats
Tremors

Lingering odor of inhalant material
Rash around the nose and mouth

Opioid painkillers

Opioids are narcotic, painkilling drugs produced from opium or made synthetically. This class of drugs includes, among others, heroin, morphine, codeine, methadone, fentanyl and oxycodone. Sometimes called the "opioid epidemic," addiction to opioid prescription pain medicines has reached an alarming rate across the United States. Some people who've been using opioids over a long period of time may need physician-prescribed temporary or long-term drug substitution during treatment.
Signs and symptoms of narcotic use and dependence can include:
A sense of feeling "high"
Reduced sense of pain
Agitation, drowsiness or sedation
Slurred speech
Problems with attention and memory
Pupils that are smaller than usual
Lack of awareness or inattention to surrounding people and things
Problems with coordination
Depression
Confusion
Constipation
Runny nose or nose sores (if snorting drugs)
Needle marks (if injecting drugs)

When to see a doctor

If your drug use is out of control or causing problems, get help. The sooner you seek help, the greater your chances for a long-term recovery. Talk with your health care provider or see a mental health provider, such as a doctor who specializes in addiction medicine or addiction psychiatry, or a licensed alcohol and drug counselor.

Make an appointment to see a provider if:

You can't stop using a drug

You continue using the drug despite the harm it causes

Your drug use has led to unsafe behavior, such as sharing needles or unprotected sex

You think you may be having withdrawal symptoms after stopping drug use

If you're not ready to approach a health care provider or mental health professional, help lines or hotlines may be a good place to learn about treatment. You can find these lines listed on the internet or in the phone book.

When to seek emergency help

Seek emergency help if you or someone you know has taken a drug and:

May have overdosed

Shows changes in consciousness

Has trouble breathing

Has seizures or convulsions

Has signs of a possible heart attack, such as chest pain or pressure

Has any other troublesome physical or psychological reaction to use of the drug

Staging an intervention

People struggling with addiction usually deny they have a problem and hesitate to seek treatment. An intervention presents a loved one with a structured opportunity to make changes before things get even worse and can motivate someone to seek or accept help.

It's important to plan an intervention carefully. It may be done by family and friends in consultation with a health care provider or mental health professional such as a licensed alcohol and drug counselor, or directed by an intervention professional. It involves family and friends and sometimes co-workers, clergy or others who care about the person struggling with addiction.

During the intervention, these people gather together to have a direct, heart-to-heart conversation with the person about the consequences of addiction. Then they ask the person to accept treatment.

Causes

Like many mental health disorders, several factors may contribute to development of drug addiction. The main factors are:

1.Environment. Environmental factors, including your family's beliefs and attitudes and exposure to a peer group that encourages drug use, seem to play a role in initial drug use.

2.Genetics. Once you've started using a drug, the development into addiction may be influenced by inherited (genetic) traits, which may delay or speed up the disease progression.

Changes in the brain

Physical addiction appears to occur when repeated use of a drug changes the way your brain feels pleasure. The addicting drug causes physical changes to some nerve cells (neurons) in your brain. Neurons use chemicals called neurotransmitters to communicate. These changes can remain long after you stop using the drug.

Risk factors

People of any age, sex or economic status can become addicted to a drug. Certain factors can affect the likelihood and speed of developing an addiction:

1.Family history of addiction. Drug addiction is more common in some families and likely involves an increased risk based on genes. If you have a blood relative, such as a parent or sibling, with alcohol or drug addiction, you're at greater risk of developing a drug addiction.

2.Mental health disorder. If you have a mental health disorder such as depression, attention-deficit/hyperactivity disorder (ADHD) or post-traumatic stress disorder, you're more likely to become addicted to drugs. Using drugs can become a way of coping with painful feelings, such as anxiety, depression and loneliness, and can make these problems even worse.

3.Peer pressure. Peer pressure is a strong factor in starting to use and misuse drugs, particularly for young people.

4.Lack of family involvement. Difficult family situations or lack of a bond with your parents or siblings may increase the risk of addiction, as can a lack of parental supervision.

5.Early use. Using drugs at an early age can cause changes in the developing brain and increase the likelihood of progressing to drug addiction.

6.Taking a highly addictive drug. Some drugs, such as stimulants, cocaine or opioid painkillers, may result in faster development of addiction than other drugs. Smoking or injecting drugs can increase the potential for addiction. Taking drugs considered less addicting — so-called "light drugs" — can start you on a pathway of drug use and addiction.

Complications

Drug use can have significant and damaging short-term and long-term effects. Taking some drugs can be particularly risky, especially if you take high doses or combine them with other drugs or alcohol. Here are some examples.

Methamphetamine, opiates and cocaine are highly addictive and cause multiple short-term and long-term health consequences, including psychotic behavior, seizures or death due to overdose. Opioid drugs affect the part of the brain that controls breathing, and overdose can result in death. Taking opioids with alcohol increases this risk.

GHB and flunitrazepam may cause sedation, confusion and memory loss. These so-called "date rape drugs" are known to impair the ability to resist unwanted contact and recollection of the event. At high doses, they can cause seizures, coma and death. The danger increases when these drugs are taken with alcohol.

MDMA — also known as molly or ecstasy — can interfere with the body's ability to regulate temperature. A severe spike in body temperature can result in liver, kidney or heart failure and death. Other complications can include severe dehydration, leading to seizures. Long-term, MDMA can damage the brain.

One particular danger of club drugs is that the liquid, pill or powder forms of these drugs available on the street often contain unknown substances that can be harmful, including other illegally manufactured or pharmaceutical drugs.

Due to the toxic nature of inhalants, users may develop brain damage of different levels of severity. Sudden death can occur even after a single exposure.

Other life-changing complications

Dependence on drugs can create a number of dangerous and damaging complications, including:

Getting an infectious disease. People who are addicted to a drug are more likely to get an infectious disease, such as HIV, either through unsafe sex or by sharing needles with others.

Other health problems. Drug addiction can lead to a range of both short-term and long-term mental and physical health problems. These depend on what drug is taken.

Accidents. People who are addicted to drugs are more likely to drive or do other dangerous activities while under the influence.

Suicide. People who are addicted to drugs die by suicide more often than people who aren't addicted.

Family problems. Behavioral changes may cause relationship or family conflict and custody issues.

Work issues. Drug use can cause declining performance at work, absenteeism and eventual loss of employment.

Problems at school. Drug use can negatively affect academic performance and motivation to excel in school.

Legal issues. Legal problems are common for drug users and can stem from buying or possessing illegal drugs, stealing to support the drug addiction, driving while under the influence of drugs or alcohol, or disputes over child custody.

Financial problems. Spending money to support drug use takes away money from other needs, could lead to debt, and can lead to illegal or unethical behaviors.

Prevention

The best way to prevent an addiction to a drug is not to take the drug at all. If your health care provider prescribes a drug with the potential for addiction, use care when taking the drug and follow instructions.

Health care providers should prescribe these medicines at safe doses and amounts and monitor their use so that you're not given too great a dose or for too long a time. If you feel you need to take more than the prescribed dose of a medicine, talk to your health care provider.

Preventing drug misuse in children and teenagers

Take these steps to help prevent drug misuse in your children and teenagers:

Communicate. Talk to your children about the risks of drug use and misuse.

Listen. Be a good listener when your children talk about peer pressure and be supportive of their efforts to resist it.

Set a good example. Don't misuse alcohol or addictive drugs. Children of parents who misuse drugs are at greater risk of drug addiction.

Strengthen the bond. Work on your relationship with your children. A strong, stable bond between you and your child will reduce your child's risk of using or misusing drugs.

Preventing a relapse

Once you've been addicted to a drug, you're at high risk of falling back into a pattern of addiction. If you do start using the drug, it's likely you'll lose control over its use again — even if you've had treatment and you haven't used the drug for some time.

Follow your treatment plan. Monitor your cravings. It may seem like you've recovered and you don't need to keep taking steps to stay drug-free. But your chances of staying drug-free will be much higher if you continue seeing your therapist or counselor, going to support group meetings and taking prescribed medicine.

Avoid high-risk situations. Don't go back to the neighborhood where you used to get your drugs. And stay away from your old drug crowd.

Get help immediately if you use the drug again. If you start using the drug again, talk to your health care provider, your mental health provider or someone else who can help you right away.

Prescription Drug Abuse

Prescription drug abuse is the use of a prescription medicine in a way not intended by the prescriber. Prescription drug abuse, also called prescription drug misuse, includes everything from taking a friend's prescription painkiller for your backache to snorting or injecting ground-up pills to get high. Prescription drug abuse may become ongoing and compulsive, despite the negative consequences.

An increasing problem, prescription drug abuse can affect all age groups, including teens. The prescription drugs most often misused include opioid painkillers, anti-anxiety medicines, sedatives and stimulants.

Early identification of prescription drug abuse and early

intervention may prevent the problem from turning into an addiction.

Symptoms

Signs and symptoms of prescription drug abuse depend on the specific drug. Because of their mind-altering properties, the most misused prescription drugs are:

Opioids used to treat pain, such as medicines containing oxycodone (Oxycontin, Percocet) and those containing hydrocodone (Norco)

Anti-anxiety medicines, sedatives and hypnotics used to treat anxiety and sleep disorders, such as alprazolam (Xanax), diazepam (Valium) and zolpidem (Ambien)

Stimulants used to treat attention-deficit/hyperactivity disorder (ADHD) and certain sleep disorders, such as methylphenidate (Ritalin, Concerta, others), dextroamphetamine-amphetamine (Adderall XR, Mydayis) and dextroamphetamine (Dexedrine)

Signs and symptoms of prescription drug abuse

Opioids
    Constipation
    Nausea
    Feeling high
    Slowed breathing rate
    Drowsiness
    Confusion
    Poor coordination
    Increased dose needed for pain relief
    Worsening or increased sensitivity to pain with higher doses
    Anti-anxiety medicines and sedatives
    Drowsiness
    Confusion
    Unsteady walking

Slurred speech
Poor concentration
Dizziness
Problems with memory
Slowed breathing
Stimulants
Increased alertness
Feeling high
Irregular heartbeat
High blood pressure
High body temperature
Reduced appetite
Insomnia
Agitation
Anxiety
Paranoia

Other signs

Forging, stealing or selling prescriptions
Taking higher doses than prescribed
Being hostile or having mood swings
Sleeping less or more
Making poor decisions
Being unusually energetic, high or revved up
Being drowsy
Requesting early refills or continually "losing" prescriptions, so more prescriptions must be written
Trying to get prescriptions from more than one prescriber

When to see a doctor

Talk with your health care provider if you think you may have a problem with prescription drug use. You may feel embarrassed to talk about it — but remember that medical professionals are trained to help you, not judge you. It's easier to face the problem early before it becomes an addiction and leads to more-serious problems.

Causes

Teens and adults abuse prescription drugs for many reasons, such as:

To feel good or get high

To relax or relieve tension

To ease pain

To reduce appetite

To increase alertness

To experiment with mental effects of the substance

To maintain an addiction and prevent withdrawal

To be accepted by peers or to be social

To try to improve concentration and school or work performance

Risk factors

Some people fear that they may become addicted to medicines prescribed for medical conditions, such as painkillers prescribed after surgery. But you can reduce your risk by carefully following your health care provider's instructions on how to take your medicine.

Prescription drug abuse is highest among teens and young adults.

Risk factors for prescription drug misuse include:

Past or present addictions to other substances, including alcohol and tobacco

Family history of substance abuse problems

Certain preexisting mental health conditions

Peer pressure or a social environment where there's drug use

Easier access to prescription drugs, such as having prescription medicines in the home medicine cabinet

Lack of knowledge about prescription drugs and their potential harm

Older adults and prescription drug abuse

Prescription drug abuse in older adults is a growing problem, especially when they combine drugs with alcohol. Having multiple health problems and taking multiple drugs can put people at risk of misusing drugs or becoming addicted.

Complications

Abusing prescription drugs can cause a number of problems. Prescription drugs can be especially dangerous — and even lead to death — when taken in high doses, when combined with other prescription drugs or certain over-the-counter medicines, or when taken with alcohol or illegal or recreational drugs.

Medical consequences

Here are examples of serious consequences of prescription drug abuse:

#Opioids# can cause a slowed breathing rate and potential for breathing to stop. Opioids can also cause coma. An overdose can lead to death.

#Anti-anxiety# medicines and sedatives — medicines to help you feel calm or less anxious — can cause memory problems, low blood pressure and slowed breathing. An overdose can cause coma or death. Abruptly stopping the medicine may cause withdrawal

symptoms that can include an overactive nervous system and seizures.

#Stimulants# can cause an increase in body temperature, heart problems, high blood pressure, seizures or tremors, hallucinations, aggressiveness, and paranoia.

Physical dependence and addiction

Because commonly abused prescription drugs activate the brain's reward center, it's possible to develop physical dependence and addiction.

#Physical dependence# Physical dependence, also called drug tolerance, is the body's response to long-term use of a drug. People who are physically dependent on a drug may need higher doses to get the same effects and may experience withdrawal symptoms when cutting back or abruptly stopping the drug.

#Addiction# People who are addicted to a drug can have physical dependence, but they also compulsively seek a drug and continue to use it even when that drug causes major problems in their lives.

Other consequences

Other potential consequences include:

Engaging in risky behaviors because of poor judgment

Using illegal or recreational drugs

Being involved in crime

Being involved in motor vehicle accidents

Showing decreased school or work performance

Having troubled relationships

Prevention

Prescription drug abuse may occur in people who need painkillers, sedatives or stimulants to treat a medical condition. If you're taking a prescription drug that commonly leads to drug misuse, here are ways to reduce your risk:

Make sure you're getting the right medicine. Make sure your health care provider clearly understands your condition and the signs and symptoms. Tell your health care provider about all your prescriptions, as well as over-the-counter medicines, herbs and supplements, and alcohol and other drug use. Ask your doctor whether there's another medicine with ingredients that have less potential for addiction.

Check in with your health care provider. Talk with your health care provider on a regular basis to make sure that the medicine is working and you're taking the right dose.

Follow directions carefully. Use your medicine the way it was prescribed. Don't stop or change the dose of a drug on your own if it doesn't seem to be working without talking to your health care provider. For example, if you're taking a pain medicine that isn't adequately controlling your pain, don't take more.

Know what your medicine does. Ask your health care provider or pharmacist about the effects of your medicine, so you know what to expect. Also check if other drugs, over-the-counter products or alcohol should be avoided when taking this medicine.

Never use another person's prescription. Everyone is different. Even if you have a similar medical condition, it may not be the right medicine or dose for you.

Don't order prescriptions online unless they're from a trustworthy pharmacy. Some websites sell counterfeit prescription and over-the-counter drugs that could be dangerous.

Preventing prescription drug abuse in teens

Prescription drugs are commonly misused substances by young people. Follow these steps to help prevent your teen from abusing prescription medicines.

Discuss the dangers. Emphasize to your teen that just because drugs are prescribed by a health care provider doesn't make them safe — especially if they were prescribed to someone else or if your child is already taking other prescription medicines.

Set rules. Let your teen know that it's not OK to share medicines with others — or to take drugs prescribed for others. Emphasize the importance of taking the prescribed dose and talking with the health care provider before making changes.

Discuss the dangers of alcohol use. Using alcohol with medicines can increase the risk of accidental overdose.

Keep your prescription drugs safe. Keep track of drug quantities and keep them in a locked medicine cabinet.

Make sure your child isn't ordering drugs online. Some websites sell counterfeit and dangerous drugs that may not require a prescription.

Properly dispose of medicines. Don't leave unused or expired drugs around. Check the label or patient information guide for disposal instructions. You can also ask your pharmacist for advice on disposal.

FIVE

Could you be Addicted to the Interenet? Internet Addiction Disorder (IAD)

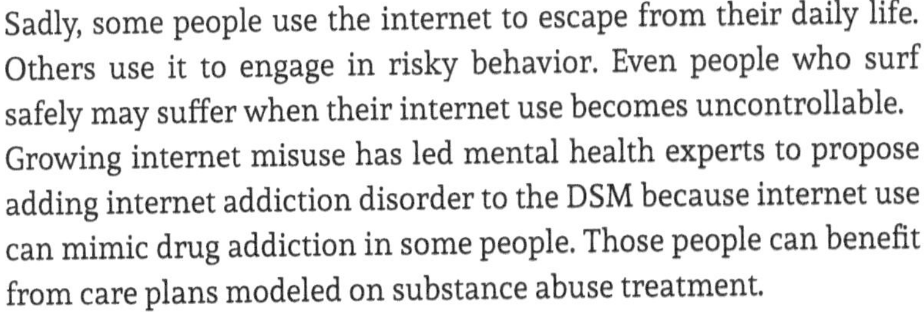

Sadly, some people use the internet to escape from their daily life. Others use it to engage in risky behavior. Even people who surf safely may suffer when their internet use becomes uncontrollable. Growing internet misuse has led mental health experts to propose adding internet addiction disorder to the DSM because internet use can mimic drug addiction in some people. Those people can benefit from care plans modeled on substance abuse treatment.

what internet Addiction is ?

Many of us are glued to our phones, our computers, or our iPads for the majority of the day, every day. Whether we're required to for work or doing so for personal pleasure. Consider a few internet use statistics:

There are more than 4.33 billion active internet users (Datareportal, 2019).

There are 3.9 billion unique mobile internet users (Statistica, 2019).

On average, internet users spend 6 hours and 30 minutes online every day. (Bond Cap, 2019).

91% visit online stores

2+ hours a day on social media; highest among Millennials and Generation X.

China has the highest amount of internet users, with over 854 million (Internetworldstats, 2019).

In the US, 81% of adults go online every single day (Pew Research, 2019).

There are over 1.7 billion websites (Internet Live Stats, 2019).

It's safe to say that the majority of us spend much of our time online, especially now during the era of COVID-19 as we desperately try to stay connected to others and keep ourselves entertained during social distancing. But we don't all suffer as a result of our internet use and time online—at least not to the degree of those with an addiction.

Internet addiction—sometimes called compulsive computer use, pathological internet use, and internet dependence—is yet to be listed in the Diagnostic and Statistical Manual of Mental Disorders (DSM). However, when engagement in a certain activity negatively impacts one's wellbeing and takes priority over important areas of life—such as work, school, and the individual's relationships—this activity can be classified as an addiction.

In simple terms, internet addiction is compulsive or frequent activity on the internet despite harmful consequences. These people are staying up all night and sleeping through their alarms. They're missing school or work, neglecting their relationships, and disregarding other responsibilities like taking a shower or paying their bills. As we mentioned above, internet addiction is not yet classified as a disorder in the DSM. But, that doesn't mean other professionals don't recognize internet addiction. Those that do acknowledge internet addiction classify it as an obsessive-compulsive disorder or impulse control disorder. And they use corresponding treatment methods to help the affected individual(s).

Internet Addiction Symptoms: Do I Have Internet Addiction?

We can all relate to watching one too many episodes on Netflix or staying up too late gaming. But this certainly doesn't mean we're addicted to the Internet, or the specific medium at hand—does it? As with other addictions, an activity becomes problematic when it negatively affects important areas of life. With that in mind, here are the emotional (or mental) symptoms of internet addiction, as well as the physical symptoms

Emotional Internet Addiction Symptoms:

Euphoria when using the internet on one's phone or computer
  Inability to prioritize schedules or manage time
  Boredom or lack of interest in routine tasks
  No sense of time
  Loneliness and isolation
  Mood swings or irritability
  Depression
  Anxiety
  Avoidance of work
  Defensiveness

Physical Internet Addiction Symptoms:

Carpal tunnel
  Headaches
  Insomnia or other sleep disturbances
  Poor nutrition and/or personal hygiene
  Significant changes in weight
  Neck and back pain
  Dry eyes, or other vision issues

There isn't a specific set of criteria one must meet to be diagnosed with internet addiction (because internet addiction isn't technically classified as a disorder in the DSM, as we've mentioned), but if you are experiencing the above symptoms with excessive internet use, you might have a problem. Additionally, you can consult the following diagnostic criteria, which was proposed by KW Beard in the journal Cyberpsychology and Behavior and well-received in the community:

1.The individual is preoccupied with the Internet, in that they are constantly thinking about using it or their past use of it

2.The individual must increase the amount of time they spend on the internet to continue gaining satisfaction

3.They have tried and failed to control, cut back on, or stop their internet use

4.They become depressed, restless, moody, or irritable as a result of trying to manage their internet use

5.The individual stays online longer than they originally intended.

Additionally, at least one of the following must be present:

"The individual has jeopardized their job, relationships, schooling, or opportunities due to their internet use

They have lied to family members, friends, and others about their internet use

The individual uses the internet to escape or avoid their problems, or to cope with difficult emotions

If you're worried about your internet habits and think that you might have internet addiction, you should talk to a medical professional. They can help you better understand whether your habits are unhealthy and what to do next."

Types of Internet Addiction

1.Computer Gaming Addiction: This type of internet addiction is what most people think of right off the bat. Computer addiction, or computer gaming addiction, simply involves activities that can be performed on a computer, both on and offline. When more and more people gained access to computers, games like Solitaire and Tetris were programmed into the computer software. These games were probably meant to be played at random and help users pass the time when bored, but they quickly became a problem.

Researchers found that people were developing computer or gaming addictions, wherein they were spending significant amounts of time playing these and other games, and suffering as a result. For example, office employees spent (and still do) too much time playing these games and their productivity, as well as their motivation at work, plummeted.As you probably know, these computer games as well as thousands of others are still available and widely played today. Computer or gaming addiction is the oldest of internet addiction types. Not to mention, it is still common if not more common today.

2.Cybersex Addiction: Cybersex addiction is comprised of online pornography, adult chat rooms and websites, and web-cam services. An obsession with any of the aforementioned can prove harmful to one's life, specifically in their relationships. An individual who is addicted to porn or another service of sexual nature often struggles to form intimate, romantic, and/or sexual relationships in real life.

3.Online Relationship Addiction: Those with an online relationship addiction are obsessed with finding and maintaining relationships online, which often leads to their neglecting in-person relationships, such as those with family members and friends.These online relationships are typically created in chat rooms or social media platforms, but can be formed anywhere online. This isn't just harmful to one's mental and emotional wellbeing—it's dangerous. Oftentimes, people who pursue relationships online do so under a fake name and persona. It's hard to know when the person you're chatting with online is telling the truth about their identity.

4.Net Compulsions: Net compulsions refer to online activities like gambling, auctioning, shopping, and trading stocks. These habits can have a negative mental, emotional, and financial impact on an individual, as losing an excessive amount of money can cause significant stress in one's life.It is easy for people to fall into the trap of net compulsions, especially those who already have a gambling, spending, or shopping addiction.

5.Compulsive Information Seeking: Compulsive information seeking is acting on that uncontrollable urge to Google (or Bing).

Some people just can't resist gathering information on the web, from the symptoms of an illness to random facts about a celebrity, how to change a tire, etc. This form of internet addiction can negatively affect one's performance at work and even lead to severe anxiety issues.

Causes of Internet Addiction; Risk Factors

As with most disorders, there isn't always a clear cause of internet addiction. However, there are likely multiple factors that contribute to the development of this disorder, some of which are rooted in nature and others that are rooted in nurture. Let's explore a few of these potential factors:

1.Dopamine chase: Many addictive drugs, like alcohol and cocaine, are linked to this elusive "dopamine chase." For example, when an individual uses their drug of choice, they experience pleasure and release dopamine, which causes them to experience euphoria. The drug user starts to chase this euphoric feeling, which reinforces their behavior. And over time, more of the drug is needed for the individual to achieve the feelings they seek.A similar cycle is seen in internet addiction: If you like to play video games or shop online, and you struggle with an internet addiction or obsession, you'll have to spend more and more time engaging in the behavior to achieve the same level of pleasure.

2.Multiple layers of rewards: Another theory, the Variable Ratio Reinforcement Schedule (VRRS) theory, says that internet addiction can stem from multiple levels of rewards. For example, your scrolling through social media might reward you many times, as you receive likes and comments on the photo you just posted, accept a friend request from your crush, and read exciting updates about your friends getting engaged or pregnant. Every time you sign on to Facebook, Instagram, or another social platform, you never know what you're going to get—but there is always potential for multiple levels of rewards, which keeps you coming back for more.

3.Chemical makeup and structural brain changes: Additionally, some research suggests that those with internet addiction have brain makeup similar to individuals with drug or alcohol dependence. Additionally, some research shows that internet addiction physically changes the structure of the brain, in that it affects gray and white matter in the prefrontal regions, which help with remembering details, planning, prioritizing, and paying attention. Therefore, when this area of the brain is altered, we aren't able to prioritize the right tasks—we prioritize the internet, instead.

4.Genetics: Your genetics might also play a role in the development of internet addiction. If you struggle with this form of addiction (or another type of addiction), your dopamine or serotonin levels might be lower than most, requiring you to engage in more behaviors to achieve the same level of pleasure. This biological predisposition can increase your risk for addiction.

5.Depression and Anxiety: Finally, if you have depression or anxiety, you are more likely to turn to the internet for relief. For example, if you suffer from social anxiety, it's much easier to meet people in a virtual world than it is to meet people face to face. These individuals find pleasure in these interactions and relationships just the same, only they must engage in them online. This can put someone on the fast road to internet addiction.

Effects of Internet Addiction: Short-Term and Long-Term

When it comes to internet addiction (and other types of addiction), there are both short-term and long-term effects, of which can prove harmful to the individual. Short-term effects include:

Incomplete tasks

Neglected responsibilities

Weight loss or gain

Backache

Neck pain

An individual with internet addiction might experience the above symptoms after only several sessions on the internet. Long-term side effects include:

Carpal tunnel syndrome

Vision problems

Damaged relationships

Loss of a job

Financial strain

When one is farther into their addiction, they are more likely to experience the above side effects. As they spend more and more time on the internet, they are at a greater risk of experiencing carpal tunnel, hurting their vision, damaging their relationships, losing their job, and entering financial distress as a result of their job loss or spending money on shopping, gambling, or gambling online.

How to Avoid internet Addiction?

Internet addiction is a common problem that can be just as damaging as any other form of addiction. If you are concerned that you may be too dependent on the internet, there are several strategies you can use to curb your internet usage. Start by limiting when you will allow yourself to use the internet, such as by keeping a diary of your internet use and specifying when you will allow yourself to log on. You can also remove the temptation to go online by shutting off devices, putting devices in another room to charge, or unplugging your wifi. Developing healthy habits can also help you to cut back on your internet use and feel better overall.

Here are some Beneficial Methods

1.Removing the Temptation to Browse

Turn off your smart phone, tablet, and computer during social activities. If your devices are on and within arm's reach, you may find yourself mindlessly checking them during meal times and other social activities. If you're spending time with family or friends, turn off your device or at least put it on silent and place it somewhere out of sight, such as in a coat pocket, in your purse, or in another room.

If you are worried about missing an urgent phone call or text, set your phone to silent, but with an exception to ring or buzz for phone calls or texts from certain contacts.

• Charge devices in another room at night to prevent bedtime browsing. If you often browse the internet on your phone while lying in bed, prevent yourself from doing this by charging your phone in another room of the house. Read a book (a paper one) or a magazine, or use a relaxation technique to help you wind down at night.

Did you know? Bedtime browsing can interfere with your ability to fall asleep and stay asleep due to the blue light that your smart phone emits, so stopping bedtime browsing may also help you to sleep better.

• Remove social media apps from your phone. If you find yourself picking up your phone and going on the internet every time you get a notification, delete the social media apps on your phone. Make it a rule that you can only check these apps on your computer. This may help to prevent you from accessing them on and off all day.

While social media apps are convenient for staying connected, they can also cause you to hop on the internet much more frequently than you normally would. You may notice a big difference in your internet habits by simply deleting the apps.

• Look at 1 website at a time instead of having multiple tabs open. If you tend to look at one website, then open another tab, then another, and another, you might benefit from limiting yourself to one tab at a time. If you are one a website and it leads you to another one, close the old tab. This can help you to avoid going back and forth between multiple sites and wasting time.

• Block time-wasting sites on your internet browser. If you want to avoid accessing sites that take up a lot of your time, you can block them by changing the settings in your internet browser. The method for this will vary depending on the type of browser you use and whether you use a phone or PC. By blocking time-wasting sites, such as social media, you may find yourself spending less time online.

• Turn off or cut your home wifi access to prevent internet use entirely. Unplug the router and set a timer for 1, 2, 3 hours, or however long you want to remain offline, then plug the wifi back in when you are ready to use it again. For a more drastic option, you could cancel your home internet access. This may be a good solution if you find yourself unable to control your urges to browse the internet, respond to emails, or check social media..

If the temptation to browse is strong and you find yourself absentmindedly logging on, always unplug your wifi router for a portion of the time you are at home. Unplugging is also a good option if you have other household members who want to cut back on their internet usage.

2. Developing Healthier Habits

• Replace internet use with a healthy activity. Exercising, reading a book, writing, studying, knitting, and doing crossword puzzles are all better alternatives to mindlessly browsing the internet. If you want to cut back on how often you are using the internet but aren't sure what to do with the extra time, identify a few activities that you enjoy and pick one to do instead when you're feeling the urge to go online.

For example, you could keep a knitting project in your purse and pick it up any time you find yourself wanting to check social media.

Or, you could keep a small paperback book with you during the day and read whenever you'd normally browse the internet.

• Use relaxation techniques to reduce stress and anxiety. Yoga, meditation, progressive muscle relaxation, and deep breathing are all great ways to relax when you're feeling stressed. Instead of reaching for your smart phone or laptop when you are feeling stressed, try using one of these techniques to calm yourself. Other strategies you might try include:

Going for a walk in nature

Calling a friend to talk

Taking a bubble bath

Engaging in a favorite hobby

Tuning into the present

• Reach out to friends and family to build more in-person connections. If you're craving social interaction, call up a friend and make plans to do something fun, or arrange a family dinner or game night. If you don't have friends or family who you can turn to, look into a special interest group that you can join. Attend in-person meetings to connect with other people who share your interests and make new friends.

Tip: Some people turn to the internet is because they feel lonely, but the internet is not a substitute for connecting with people in-person. Make sure to balance your virtual socializing with in-person socializing.

• Watch for signs of internet addiction and seek help if you notice them. If you are concerned about becoming addicted to the internet, staying aware of the signs of internet addiction may help you know when to seek help. Be on the lookout for any signs that you may have become addicted and act right away to curb your internet usage. If strategies to overcome internet addiction don't work for you, talk with your doctor or a therapist for help. You may be addicted to the internet if:

Internet usage interferes with your normal daily activities, such as making you late for appointments, school, or work.

Staying up late browsing the internet becomes the norm and you get less sleep as a result.

You find it difficult to focus on other tasks, such as work or school assignments, because you keep logging on to check things.

Cutting back on your internet use makes you feel irritated or anxious.

You withdraw from social activities and lose interest in doing things you use to enjoy.

You feel worried that you might miss out on something if you don't check the internet regularly.

3.Tracking and Limiting Internet Use

SIX
HOW TO BEAT AN ADDICTION TO CELL PHONES

Do you find yourself constantly texting, surfing the internet, sending emails, using applications and playing games? Depending on how much time and effort you put into those situations, you may have a problem with excessive cell phone use. Overuse of your cell phone can lead to reduced quality of personal relationships and lack of productivity in daily life.

1. Going on a Cell Phone Diet

Monitor your cell phone use. According to one study, college students may spend 8-10 hours per day on their cell phones. Tracking your cell phone use such as adding up how many times per hour you check your phone can increase your awareness about your problem. If you are aware of the extent of your problem you can begin to identify goals and possible solutions.

Try downloading an application that tracks your cell phone use like Checky, App Off Timer, or QualityTime.You can use this information to set a specific goal of how many times per hour or day you allow yourself to check your phone.

• Create a plan for your phone use. Limit your cell phone use to certain times of the day. You can set an alarm on your phone to alert you when you have reached your maximum time. For example, you can allow yourself to use your phone only from 6PM-7PM. You can also set up specific times not to use your phone, such as while you are at work or school.

Write your plan and goals down to make them more concrete. Keep a log of which goals you've met and ones you are still working on.

•Offer yourself rewards for less time spent on your phone. This concept is called positive self-reinforcement and it is used in therapy in order to teach an individual positive behaviors through the use of a reward system. For example, if you meet your cell phone use goal for the day you can treat yourself to your favorite food, a new item, or an activity.

• Start slow. Instead of going cold turkey and completely eliminating your cell phone use (which can be very anxiety-provoking), begin by progressively reducing the amount of time you spend checking your phone. For example, start by limiting the amount you check your phone to once per 30 minutes, then once per 2 hours, as so on.

Keep a tally of how many times you check your phone per hour.

Use your phone only for necessary communications or emergencies.

• Put your phone away. Put your phone somewhere where you will not see it. Turn your phone on silent mode when you are at work, study or anywhere else, so it won't distract you.

• Take a cell phone holiday. Cut cell phone use out of your life completely for a short period of time such as a weekend.

Go on a trip or camping where there will be no cell service. This forces you to be off of your phone.

You can notify your friends and loved ones that you are going off the grid for a short time. This can be easily accomplished on social media.

• Change your phone settings. There are settings on your phone that may alert you every time you get an email or Facebook notification. Make sure you turn these off! This will reduce the number of times your phone goes off or vibrates. This way you are not being notified every time something occurs.

Settle for a pay-as-you-go plan as a last resort. It's similar to a portable payphone and a calling card in one - in order to use a certain amount of minutes, you'll need to pay for that amount. It then disables your phone when you reach the maximum of minutes.

• Change your thinking about your cell phone. Changing your thoughts may help alter your emotions and behaviors. In other words, if you change your thinking about your cell phone you can feel better and use your cell phone less.

Remind yourself that whatever you are wanting to check on your phone is not that important and can wait.

Next time you feel the need to use it step back and think, "Do I really need to call/text this person right now or can it wait until later?

• Focus on the here-and-now. Mindfulness, the art of being aware, can help you become centered and possibly reduce the impulse to engage in cell phone use. Try to be in the present moment by focusing on what is currently going on, including your own thoughts and reactions.

2. Considering Alternatives to Using Your Cell Phone

• Understand your triggers to phone use. Triggers are your feelings and thoughts about a situation that leads to a certain behavior (cell phone use). Learning why you are urged to use your cell phone can help you develop alternative options.

Are you on your cell phone because you have a strong desire to be social and connect with others? If so, you can fulfill your needs in ways that last longer such as face-to-face contact.

Are you simply bored? Boredom can be a huge trigger for individuals to engage in addictive behaviors. If you are often bored, it may be time to develop hobbies or other activities that sustain your attention.

• Engage in other mood-boosting activities. Using your cell phone has been linked to increases in mood, which positively reinforces cell phone use. Instead of using your phone to feel better, engage in alternative activities such as exercise/sports or creative activities such as writing or drawing.

• Keep busy! If you have a specific plan for each day and you are focusing on your responsibilities, you will have less time to spend on your phone. The bonus is that you will spend more time focusing on your goals and being productive.

If you are not employed you can apply to jobs or volunteer at a local organization.

Try taking up a new hobby like knitting, sewing or playing an instrument.

Spend more time doing things that need to be finished, whether it's chores or parents wanting a family day or time together.

• Redirect your attention by doing something constructive. Try to do something constructive instead of using your phone the next time you feel the urge. Focus on your own personal goals and objectives for the day. Make a list of tasks that do not involve your phone and any time you have the impulse to check your phone, stop and gently redirect your attention to your responsibilities.

• Accomplish social tasks in a different way. Much of our desire to be on the phone comes from our innate and evolutionary drive to be social beings. However, there are other options to be social which may be more beneficial and satisfying in the long-term.

Instead of texting, write a letter or meet up with a friend for coffee or a meal.

Instead of blasting your photos on Instagram, invite a family member over and physically show them your memories. This type of connection may increase quality intimacy.

• Replace your habits. Think of each reason you use your cell phone (games, texting, phone calls). Some of these habits may be necessary to your work and daily life (perhaps work emails, etc), while others could be disrupting your life if they take away from your normal interactions and responsibilities. Attempt to replace each of these disruptive habits into more productive, social, and quality experiences.

If one of your issues is excessively playing games on your phone, think of an alternative such as inviting a friend over to play a board game.

If you spend too much time looking at profiles on social media, meet up with a close friend or family member and ask them about what is going on in their life (instead of simply reading about it online).

3. Getting Support

• Notify people about your issue. Social support is a crucial component of mental health. Having a positive social network produces feelings of safety and connectedness. These components are important when considering limiting your cell phone use since your use is likely to be at least partly based on social connection (such as texting, using social applications). While cell phone use may feel positive, it can actually limit us and close us off from intimate relationships.

Simply tell your family and friends that you think you are using your cell phone too much and you are working on cutting down. You can explain that you would appreciate if they support you in this process. Additionally, you could give them specific suggestions and involve them in your plan. For example, ask them to call or text you only at certain times of the day.

Ask for advice. Your family members know you personally and may be able to help you devise a specific plan on cutting down your phone use.

• Ask for understanding. Let your family and friends know that you may not text, call, or email them back right away since you are attempting to cut down your cell phone use. If they are aware of the situation they are more likely to be understanding and not be upset.

• Plan face-to-face meetings. Instead of getting social support mostly through your cell phone, it is important to engage in a personal and intimate level. This can only be fully accomplished in person.

Plan an activity with family or friends. Spend your limited cell phone time researching and planning this event. This way your energy is being used in a productive and meaningful way.

• Give your cell phone to someone else. This can be especially helpful during times when you feel strong urges to use your phone including after school, after dinner, and during the weekend.

•Consider treatment. While cell phone addiction is not yet a widely recognized diagnosis, this does not mean that you cannot get help. There are treatment centers and counselors that specialize in these types of issues. If your cell phone problem is severe and disrupts your daily life and functioning, counseling or mental health treatment may be helpful.

Some signs that you may need help are if you are unable to complete your responsibilities (work, school, home), or if your interpersonal relationships are significantly negatively affected by your cell phone use.

Cognitive Behavioral Therapy (CBT) is a type of treatment that is used for a wide variety of conditions and addictions. It focuses on changing your thoughts in order to change your feelings and behaviors. CBT may be a helpful option if you choose to seek treatment.

SEVEN

IS TELEVISION AND SCREEN ADDICTION REAL

Television addiction can be seen as an addiction model which is associated with compulsive behavior, associated with watching any television programming. Television addiction is extremely difficult to control in many cases and has parallels to various other forms of behavioral addiction such as gambling or drugs. In order to understand the television addiction model in depth, we first need to understand each of the above scientific terms used. Addiction is a brain disorder which is characterized by compulsive engagement in rewarding stimuli, despite adverse consequences. Behavioral addiction is a form of addiction. The person indulges in a rewarding non-drug related behavior, though it might negatively affect the person's mental, physical, social or financial well-being. Television addiction can be with respect to any television program, or series. Further, television addiction is not a diagnosable condition of DSM-4. Further, mild hypnotism can also be deducted in a television addict.

History of TV Addiction

The idea of television addiction is nothing new and predates the explosion in media and screens of recent years. Worry over too much TV has been conceptualized and discussed since the 1970s, well before some of the behavioral addictions that have since overtaken it in terms of scientific research and widespread acceptance, such as internet addiction. Although early research into TV addiction was limited, the concept of TV addiction was relatively well accepted by parents, educators, and journalists, as television watching became more common, particularly among children.Much of the research on screentime has been devoted to its impact on children but, as we all are aware, adults are also prone to overuse.

Screen-Overload

Doctors, teachers, counselors, parents, and even kids are growingly concerned as the quantity of content, types of available media, proliferation of electronic devices, and time spent on screens all soar. According to data in Common Sense Media's 2019 "The Common Sense Census: Media Use by Tweens and Teens," the average teen spends 7 hours, 22 minutes on screens daily—not including for school or homework.

Time in front of screens is up significantly from the last survey in 2015, which is even more alarming when you consider that the American Academy of Pediatrics (AAP) recommends significantly less screentime than kids are getting.

In 2001, the AAP, citing concerns over possible links of excess screentime to aggressive behavior, poor body image, obesity, and decreased school performance, set a guideline of two hours of screentime maximum for children aged 2 and older and no screens for those under 2.5 In 2016, those guidelines were reduced to one hour for children aged 2 to 5, and more open-ended "consistent limits" were recommended for kids 6 and up, along with the advice to implement age-appropriate supervision and to teach children media-savvy skills.

Clearly, today's children are far surpassing the recommended limits. Smartphone ownership has also increased sharply with 69% of 12-year-olds now having a phone in their pockets, compared with just 41% in 2015. Today, nearly 90% of high schoolers and over 50% of 11-year-olds are smartphone owners as well.

When TV and Screentime Is a Problem

As we all know, if you have a smartphone (or any other electronic device), you also have the potential for 24-hour access to television and other content via streaming. While overuse is all too common, the relative ability or inability to self-regulate viewing time and choosing screentime to the exclusion of other activities is a key indicator of a problem.

Common Sense Media research found that tweens and teens spend the majority of their screentime binge-watching TV and videos, with YouTube and Netflix topping the most used content providers. After TV, the most frequent electronic activities among teens are gaming and social media.

According to 2019 Common Sense Media data, teens spend 39% of their over 7 daily screentime hours watching TV and videos, 22% devoted to gaming, and 16% to social media. This adds up to over 5.5 hours total and nearly 3 hours a day watching content. Tweens, who average just under 5 hours of daily screen time, allot 53% of their media time to TV and videos, 31% to gaming, and 4% to social media.

Symptoms of Television Addiction

When TV addiction was first studied in the 1970s, it was described as paralleling five of the seven DSM criteria used for diagnosing substance dependence. People who were "addicted" to television spent large amounts of their time watching it; they watched TV longer or more often than they intended; they made repeated unsuccessful efforts to cut down their TV watching; they withdrew from or gave up important social, family, or occupational activities in order to watch television; and they reported "withdrawal"-like symptoms of subjective discomfort when deprived of TV.

Studies conducted with self-identified "TV addicts" have shown that those who consider themselves addicted to television are more generally unhappy, anxious, and withdrawn than other people who watch television. These people use television watching to distract themselves from negative moods, worries and fears, and boredom. They are also somewhat more likely to be solitary and hostile and to withdraw from or have difficulty maintaining social connections with others, although it is unclear whether there is a causal link between these personality characteristics and addiction.

More recently, research shows there is a growing popular trend toward binge-watching television in our culture, which may be exacerbating television addiction. Characteristics that have been associated with self-identified TV addiction are binge-watching, susceptibility to boredom, and the use of TV to fill time. The TV (whether streaming on a device or watching on a traditional TV) is used as a way to avoid rather than seek out stimulation. In addition, people who become addicted to TV tend to have poor attention and self-control, feel guilty about wasting time, and are prone to daydreams involving fear of failure.

The Research Lag

One reason TV or screen addiction isn't considered a true addiction is a lack of sufficient research and the fact that many symptoms of overuse have been normalized. Most of us partake in some of these behaviors to some degree, from spending a weekend binge-watching our favorite show to winding down with a few hours on Facebook, YouTube, or game consoles.Everywhere we look people are staring at screens and, if not, are holding them in their hands, pockets, or bags.

However, while the research data hasn't caught up quite yet to our rapidly changing media and screen landscape, it will soon. Many studies are now in the works that should shed light on the impact all this screentime is having and whether obsessive behaviors around TV watching, social media, gaming, and/or any other electronically-based activity should be classified as true addictions. Regardless, there is a vast agreement that chronic TV watching and screen overuse is a problem.

One pertinent study is the National Institute on Drug Abuse's ongoing, large scale Longitudinal Study of Adolescent Brain Cognitive Development (ABCD Study) project. The ABCD Study, which began in 2016, is following nearly 12,000 youth over 10 years to determine the effects of screentime on brain development, among other social and environmental factors.

The one electronic activity addiction that has gained official legitimacy is gaming addiction, which was listed as a potential disorder in need of further research in the DSM-

Risks of TV Addiction

Risks of TV Addiction

Alarmingly, rates of many mental health concerns, from attention deficit hyperactivity disorder (ADHD) to suicide, are also on the rise—and some wonder if this may be, in part, related to skyrocketing screentime. In fact, a 2018 study in Pediatrics, found a link between screentime, quantity of sleep, and impulsivity-related disorders.These findings echo what many parents and experts see as a link between screens and the exacerbation of ADHD symptoms and other behavioral and mental health issues in children.

Research has also revealed disturbing evidence that excessive TV watching is associated with a shorter lifespan. Those in the highest risk category watched an average of six hours of television a day and had a lifespan nearly five years shorter than people who did not watch TV. But does TV itself cause a shorter lifespan? Perhaps not. The study's authors have stated that the results may be caused by other factors strongly associated with excessive TV watching such as overeating, lack of exercise, and depression.

Indeed, there are multiple addictive behaviors that lend themselves to hours of TV watching. Marijuana addiction and heroin addiction both tend to lead to hours of inactivity, often in front of screens. People with chronic pain who are reliant on painkillers are often limited in their mobility so they can't get out and about. And while the focus of research into shopping addiction tends to be retail stores and online shopping, it may neglect one of the most compulsive scenarios for the shopaholic—the shopping channel.

Television may be addictive, along with other forms of media, such as video game addiction, internet addiction, cybersex, and smartphone addiction. Still, it seems likely that it co-exists with many other addictions that feed off the isolation that is felt by people with numerous other behavioral and substance addictions.

So what we can do How to Overcome Television Addiction

There is nothing you want to watch on TV, yet you flip mindlessly through the channels, searching, searching for anything that might remotely catch your interest.

You know you have other things you should be doing but... just one more show, one more episode even though you've probably already seen it before.

You're bored, you're restless. There's that nagging doubt in the back of your mind that there must be more to life than this.

It's like you've lost control of your life and you're helpless to stop watching.

What's going on?

Is it that you lack willpower?

No. It's called TV addiction.

You want to stop watching, yet it keeps calling you back and the hours simply disappear and you realize you can't even remember what you saw or what happened during the episode.

You really want to stop, but how?

How do you overcome TV addiction and get back into living a life you actually enjoy?

The truth:

You need to wake up.

It's not about willpower or being strong enough to quit cold turkey. Those are important but it's not addressing the real cause of your TV addiction.

You need to change your brain from being passive to being active. TV puts your mind into a passive, trance-like state and it interferes with your ability to make clear decisions.

You might be wondering right now what TV addiction has to do with living a life of confidence, well, let me ask you this: If you're spending all your time watching TV watching other people live their lives, who's living your life?

To have a life of confidence, you need to live your life, not just watch it on TV.

So, you're now ready to make that change.

Let's take a closer look at how you can make it work this time.

How To Overcome TV Addiction

Here's what you need to know. These are 22 powerful and original ways to regain control over your life and overcome watching too much TV.

Technique #1 - Create Clarity In Your Mind

The most important part of making any change is having the sudden realization that you no longer want something in your life. So, why don't you want TV controlling your life anymore? It could simply be that you've had enough. First, make the decision you want to change. Then make the decision to choose something different for yourself.

Be determined about this change. Don't be wishy-washy about it or think, "It might be a good thing to do". Be clear with yourself that now is the time to make a change for the better. You're ready to do this. You want to do this. Be determined that it's going to work this time.

Technique #2 - Have a Reason (Educate Yourself)

Understand what TV does to your brain. It puts you into a trance and alters your brain waves. Here's a good article to explain this in detail: The Effects of TV On Your Brain

It also affects your intelligence and your ability to think. That's a chilling thought.

There's also studies that show that TV makes you far more unhappy and dissatisfied with your life.

Children's Health

"A long term study on the impact of TV on ADHD development was recently published.

Researchers in New Zealand found that kids who watched more than 2 hours of TV per day between ages 5 to 11 were significantly more likely to develop symptoms of attention deficit disorder (ADHD) than those who watched less.

"Those who watched more than two hours, and particularly those who watched more than three hours, of television per day during childhood had above-average symptoms of attention problems in adolescence," Carl Landhuis of the University of Otago in Dunedin wrote in his report, published in the journal Pediatrics.

Young children who watched a lot of television were more likely to continue the habit as they got older, but even if they did not the damage was done, the report said.

Hence, children who watch a lot of television may become less tolerant of slower-paced and more mundane tasks, such as school work," the researchers wrote."

Behavior Problems

\Other research also shows that TV can cause behavior problems in children.
If it's doing all that to children's brains, it's affecting your brain too.

Health Issues

It can also cause health problems with an increase in the risk of getting diabetes or heart disease. They say it can even shorten your life.Another recent study found that watching the news can increase people's levels of stress, anxiety and fear.
Once you know all the potential negative effects, you're less likely to see TV as an innocent past time.

Technique #3 - Appreciate The Benefits

Besides helping your brain and your health, there are numerous other reasons why you might want to make this change and overcome your TV addiction.
Just some of the benefits you'll probably discover after you stop watching so much TV are:

You'll have more free time

You'll get more rest because you're not staying up too late. This will lead to not feeling so tired and being able to cope better with your daily life.

Your schedule will become more open to new activities

You'll get more done because you'll suddenly find you have a lot more time

You'll feel better about yourself

You'll feel less anxious

You'll save money by not being exposed to so many commercials encouraging you to buy things you don't need

You'll feel more confident

Your self-esteem will rise

You'll have more energy

You'll get excited about your life again

You'll stop feeling so lethargic and sluggish

You'll find you develop clearer thinking

You'll have increased creativity

You'll be able to make headway on a dream you have because you'll finally have time to work on it

It'll help you to stop being in a fractured state all the time which promotes happiness

There are a ton of benefits to cutting out, or at least reducing your TV consumption. There's also very few negatives to stopping it.

Technique #4 - Have A Plan

Have a plan as to what you're going to do instead of watching.

Are you going to:

read more books

go for walks

join a club

work on a hobby you enjoy

meet up with some friends

call up a friend

talk to your neighbors

try a new sport

play board games

do some stretching or other exercise?

If you don't have a plan then you'll most likely drift into whatever catches your immediate attention like reading your Facebook posts or Instagram. Or the worst option of all would be to start watching YouTube videos. YouTube can be even more addicting than TV so be aware of what you're going to do instead.

I found when I first decided to go a week without any TV that I drifted into emailing people and thus was still sitting in front of a screen which isn't what I wanted.

You need to be intentional with your time. Even if that intention is to explore more things that interest you.

Technique #5 - Know Your Triggers

Habits are often triggered by the act of doing something. For example, you brush your teeth after you eat breakfast or before you go to bed.

So, if your TV has become a mindless habit for you, then you need to figure out what's the trigger for you to turn it on? Do you normally turn on the TV as soon as you walk in the door from work?

Also consider what situations trigger your desire to watch TV? Is it when you're feeling overwhelmed or when you want to procrastinate?

Once you become aware of what the trigger is for you to turn on the TV then you can break that trigger by doing something else at that time. For example, instead of turning it on as soon as you get home, you could make yourself a calming cup of tea or put on some music.

Technique #6 - Prepare For Temptation

Even though you feel strong and determined whenever you start something new, there will come a time when the old pull to watch TV will hit:

It might be a time when you feel tired... or bored... or lonely... when suddenly your head imagines how nice it would be to flop down on the couch and completely veg out.

It's going to happen at some point. So, prepare for it before it hits. Have a plan in place as to what you'll do when the TV's siren song begins. Or what will your plan be when you go stay with family and they want to sit and watch TV all night? What will you do instead?

Technique #7 - Address The Fear of Missing Out

You may feel like you're missing out somehow if you cut out the TV. Everyone else is doing something and you want to be part of the group. If all your friends and family are watching the same show, it can make you feel connected to them if you discuss the latest episode with them. Once you stop, you might feel isolated.

You could start telling them about all the things you now have time to do and what you're experiencing. You'll be demonstrating there are other options besides sitting at home doing nothing, gaining nothing.

Technique #8 - Calm Yourself, It's not NEVER

Never can be a terrifying word. Sometimes the thought "I can never watch tv again" can actually increase the pull back into that bad habit. You don't have to think in terms of 'never'.

The goal is to regain control over how you're spending your time. You may end up watching TV again every once in awhile. And, even if you do watch it occasionally, the point is that you're still making positive steps forward to regaining control over your life. You're still very much aware that you no longer want to spend all your time staring at the TV screen.

You can still be a non TV watcher and watch the occasional show. Quite likely as you go through this experiment, you might watch one or two more shows here and there as the habit fades. It's entirely up to you.

Technique #9 - Use This Quote

Here's a great quote by Epictetus.

""Whenever you get an impression of some pleasure, as with any impression,guard yourself from being carried away by it, let it await your action, give yourself pause.

After that, bring to mind both times, first when you have enjoyed the pleasure and later when you will regret and hate yourself.

Then compare to the joy and satisfaction you'd feel for abstaining altogether.

However, if a seemingly appropriate time arises to act on it, don't be overcome by its comfort, pleasantness, and allure - but against all of this, how much better the consciousness of conquering it.""

I came across this quote in the book, The Daily Stoic: 366 Meditations on Wisdom, Perseverance, and the Art of Living..........
The book adds to this quote, "It's important to connect the so-called temptation with its actual effects. Once you understand that indulging might actually be worse than resisting, the urge begins to lose its appeal. In this way, self-control becomes the real pleasure, and the temptation becomes the regret".
This is a valuable strategy to overcome any bad habit.
When temptation hits, think it through before you indulge. Do you really want to do it knowing how you'll end up feeling afterwards? Make conscious decisions for yourself. Don't just mindlessly turn the tv on.

Technique #10 - See The TV As A Bully

Who you are is distinct from what you do (your behavior). Yet you're always fully responsible for your behavior. So, if you're addicted to TV, or anything else, it's common to think of it as "your addiction". Something that's part of you.
Instead, see it as something outside yourself. It's your behavior. It's not your core inner identity means if you see this behavior as outside yourself then it becomes easier to detach from it. The

battle with yourself isn't quite so hard if what you're fighting is not seen as something inside you. You could describe TV watching as a 'parasite', or a 'con man' - something that tries to 'con' you into poisoning your mind. Whatever word you use, it'll allow you to see your TV watching as separate from who you fundamentally are.

If you think of watching TV as, "I just can't help it", then turn this around and see it as the TV is bullying you or tricking you. Changing your perspective like this can help because if someone is trying to force you to do something you don't want to do, it feels much less internally compelling and may even put you off doing it.

By describing the behavior as external to you, something that is 'bullying' you, then you realize you can 'stand up to it'.

Try seeing the TV as controlling you or abusing you. See if that changes how you feel about it.

It's something being done to you and you have the choice to choose something different.

Technique #11 - Change Your Focus

You don't spend your day thinking about all the things you don't do. For example, you don't think, "I don't cross the road without looking". Instead you look both ways before crossing the road. It's simply something you do. And, in the future, you might forget one day and cross without looking but that isn't what matters. What matters is that you're more focused on what you do in the present. That's what's important to you.

Where I'm going with this is that the temptation may be to focus on the fact that you're not watching TV. This is the wrong thing to focus on because the more you focus on it, the more you'll be drawn to it.

So, it's far more beneficial to focus on the things you are doing now instead of watching TV. You're spending more time having conversations with people, you're enjoying time spent on a hobby, you're reading more fascinating books. You don't need to waste energy thinking about what you no longer do. By doing this, you'll be more focused on what you're currently enjoying instead of how much TV you watch.

Technique #12 - Change Your Words

If you see yourself as "denying" yourself something, you're far more likely to fail at it. So, if you tell yourself you're denying yourself TV, it'll make you feel bad. If you see it as "freeing" yourself from TV, you're more likely to be successful. Or if you see it as choosing not to watch TV, you'll feel more empowered.
So, if you're feeling pulled towards the TV, pay attention to what you're telling yourself. Are you being denied something you want or are you choosing something better for yourself?

Technique #13 - Embrace The Good Feelings

Pay attention to how you feel after you've gone a couple of days of not watching TV.
See how much clearer your thinking becomes, how much calmer and relaxed you feel.
Notice how you feel less anxious and frightened by the world around you.
Appreciate how much more time you suddenly have available in your life to do what you want.

Technique #14 - Understand Your Why

Have you ever thought about why you're really watching TV? What do you get out of it besides the chance to chill out? I wrote another article about all the reasons you may not realize you're using TV for. You can check it out here: The Bad Habit of TV - What are you really using it for?
If you understand why you act and react in a certain way, then you gain the ability to choose your response rather than reacting on

automatic pilot. It's about becoming aware of the emotions behind your actions.

Technique #15 - Believe In Yourself (You're Worth It)

At first, some of your friends or family might not understand why you're doing this. They may even disapprove of what you're doing. They'll try to get you back into watching TV with them. Or your friends might get annoyed that they can't talk about the latest episode of Survivor with you.

Stay strong and believe in yourself. You know your actions are going to be beneficial to you in the end rather than getting sucked back into doing things you don't want to do.

Think of other things you can discuss with them. You could also encourage them to join you in your new activities.

Most likely after a few comments, they'll be distracted by other things and won't care whether you're watching TV or not. Your life is worth enduring a few comments by people who don't understand how important this is to you.

Remind yourself of all the benefits you're gaining from doing this. You need to be brave enough to live the life you want.

Technique #16 - Eat At Your Dinner Table

CBS News ran an article which said, "33 percent of viewers say the TV is always on during their dinner, with 27 percent saying it's on half the time, or sometimes."

One of the triggers I discovered was that when I ate dinner in front of the TV, I would then remain there for the rest of the evening watching show after show. I didn't have the willpower to turn it off once it was on.

Once I realized this then I started to eat at the dinner table. This meant that I no longer got sucked into watching the TV for the rest of the night.

The other interesting thing I discovered was that I started eating less after I made this one small change. When I ate in front of the TV, I wasn't conscious of how much I was eating and also I didn't enjoy my food anywhere near as much as when the TV is off. My brain didn't know when it was satisfied because it was focused on the TV show. Plus, I tended to watch a lot of cooking shows which would then give me the desire to eat too.

The other awesome thing that happens when you don't have the TV on during dinner is that you'll start having real conversations with those you're with rather than feeling like you can only talk during the commercials.

Technique #17 - You Make The Rules

Make rules for yourself like:

- You'll choose one show to watch and once it's over, you turn off the TV.
- You won't engage in channel surfing. • You'll be intentional about what you watch instead of random.
- You won't eat meals in front of it. • You'll set the TV's timer so it automatically turns off after an hour.

It's about making rules that demonstrate you're in control of your TV watching, and not the other way around.

Technique #18 - Become Curious

As Judson Brewer explains in his TED talk on a simple way to break bad habits, if you become curious about your behavior, you become more mindful about what you're doing. If you're mindful then you're able to more easily overcome bad habits. But the key is to first become curious about how you're feeling and how you respond to those feelings. Another fascinating video on addiction is this one by Johann Hari. His theory is that addiction is due to a loss of connection and bonding with others. So your addiction to TV may be because you're feeling disconnected from those around you.

Worth watching.

Technique #19 - Develop Better Relaxation Techniques

The most common reason I hear from people as to why they watch TV is because they want to relax or "chill out" for a bit. They say they've had a hard day and they need some downtime.

I get it. I'm the same. I also used those excuses for years.

If you've ever gone even a day without watching any TV, you'll realize that you really aren't all that relaxed after watching it. You'll be "deadened" and "mindless" but you're not relaxed and recharged and raring to go do something else which is what you said you wanted from watching TV.

I found I would feel wired or bored or restless after watching hours of it. I definitely wasn't feeling calm and relaxed.

So, find other ways to relax. Even drinking a warm cup of tea and listening to some calming music will relax you far more than watching the TV for hours.

It's about figuring out what does relax you. Maybe working on puzzles or doing some yoga or a hobby or getting out into nature. It's good to zone out and disconnect from the world sometimes. You just need to figure out some healthy ways to do it.

> "When your mind calms, you become aware of your priorities. You have a clear answer to the most important thing.
>
> If you are nervous, restless and anxious, you wake up in the morning, jump from bed and rush to the TV to listen to the news about recent elections, for example.
>
> But if your mind is calm, you feel content and you might choose to walk in the park, to enjoy nature, spend time away from the noise made by civilization"
>
> *The Art of Emptying The Brain: Nepalese method spontaneous mental healing*"

Technique #20 - Think of It As An Experiment

You don't have to continue never watching TV, if you don't want to. Think of it as an experiment though to see what it's like changing one of your mindless routines.

To conduct a true experiment, you need to do it for a certain length of time, not forever. So, you could try it as a one week experiment. After you've reached one week, make it two. After two weeks, how about trying it for a month?

Technique #21 - Start Small

It can be daunting thinking that you're giving up anything completely. So, start small. Tell yourself you'll try giving it up completely for one day. That's something that's doable.

Once you've mastered that then try two days. Keep working up and maybe the next challenge will be to go for a week. Keep building up the length of time you go for.

I've read in a number of other articles where they recommend giving up TV for at least a month. Just the thought of that sounds daunting and overwhelming. I started with a small goal of giving it up for 2 days. I was pretty sure I could do that. Once I'd done that, I then expanded the time. It became more of a game for myself. I could do it for 2 days, so how much longer could I do it for?

Technique #22 - Know Your Demons

One of the main reasons we tend to use distractions like TV is because we're avoiding dealing with our inner demons. Instead of dealing with the fact that you hate your job or you're terribly unhappy in your relationship, you'll drown out those negative feelings by numbing yourself with the TV.

Another common reason for blanking out in front of the TV is because you may be dealing with the issue of overwhelm.

It'd be far better to face your demons or at least develop better coping skills.

Or you may be suffering from soul loss and need to do a soul retrieval.

One reason I spent years staring blankly at the TV screen was because I was so terribly tired all the time. It turned out that was partly due to my thyroid not working properly. So, if you're tired all the time, figure out the reason why that's happening rather than ignoring it.

The point is you need to ensure you're not using the TV to numb your emotions or to avoid dealing with a situation. If you are, then find the solution to your issue so you can get back to living your life.

BONUS - Technique #23 - Imagine The Consequences of Not Taking Action

The easiest thing for you to do at this point would be to close this article and go flop on your couch in front of the TV.

What if instead, you take a moment and think about what you could lose by not taking control of your TV habit?

How many days of your life are you going to lose? If you only watch 3 hours per day that's still 24 hours after a week. One entire day in every week is spent watching TV. In a year, that would be 52 days spent watching TV. Almost 2 months of your life. What else could you have done in that amount of time?

So, what is the result in 3 months, or 6 months or even a year, if you do nothing? How much more could you have done in that time, if you'd simply never turned the TV on?

You have nothing to lose by trying this experiment. On the other hand, by trying this experiment you could gain a meaningful and joyful life.

This is also something entirely within your power. It's your choice. Choose wisely.

You Can Overcome Your TV Addiction

You might find it easy to quit TV or you might find it takes more work. Either way, you make it harder on yourself if you think you have to simply accept TV as part of your life. That there's nothing you can do about it.

Don't let your life slip away staring at a screen.

Take a chance and choose to start living your life and having meaningful experiences.

Use one or all of the methods above and experiment with what works for you.

You can overcome your addiction. You deserve more than this and you can do it.

Start by making the decision you want to make a change.

Choose to do something different.

Choose to turn off the TV.

You won't regret it.

EIGHT

ALCOHAL ADDICTION (AUD- ALCOHAL USE DISORDER)

Alcohol addiction is a chronic relapsing disorder associated with compulsive alcohol drinking, the loss of control over intake, and the emergence of a negative emotional state when alcohol is no longer available. Alcohol use disorder (AUD) is a condition characterized by an impaired ability to stop or control alcohol use despite adverse social, occupational, or health consequences. It is a spectrum disorder and can be mild, moderate, or severe and encompasses the conditions that some people refer to as alcohol abuse, alcohol dependence, or the colloquial term, alcoholism. Alcohol addiction refers to the moderate to severe end of the AUD spectrum..

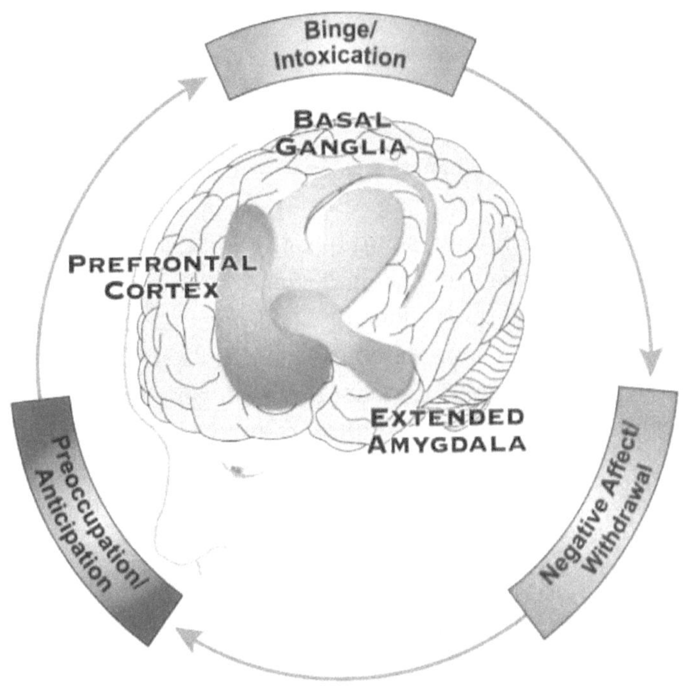

Alcohol, like other drugs, has a powerful effect on the brain, producing pleasurable feelings and blunting negative feelings. These feelings can motivate some people to drink alcohol again and again, despite possible risks to their health and well-being. For example, research shows that over time, drinking to cope with stress—while it may provide temporary relief from emotional discomfort—tends to enhance negative emotional states between bouts of alcohol consumption. These changes can motivate further drinking and cause an individual to become stuck in an unhealthy cycle of alcohol consumption.

As individuals continue to drink alcohol over time, progressive changes may occur in the structure and function of their brains. These changes can compromise brain function and drive the transition from controlled, occasional use to chronic misuse, which can be difficult to control. The changes can endure long after a person stops consuming alcohol, and can contribute to relapse in drinking.

Stages of the Addiction Cycle

Addiction can be framed as a repeating cycle, with three stages. Each stage is linked to and feeds on the others. These stages primarily involve three domains: incentive salience, negative emotional states, and executive function. The domains are reflected in three key regions of the brain: the basal ganglia, the extended amygdala, and the prefrontal cortex, respectively. A person may go through this three-stage cycle over the course of weeks or months, or progress through it several times in a day. Note also that a person can enter the cycle of addiction at any one of the following stages:

1. Binge/Intoxication Stage: reward, incentive salience, and pathological habits

During this stage, a person experiences the rewarding effects of alcohol, such as euphoria, the reduction of anxiety, and the easing of social interactions.

Repeated activation of the basal ganglia's reward system reinforces alcohol drinking behavior, increasing the likelihood of repeated consumption. The basal ganglia play an important role in motivation as well as in the formation of habits and other routine behaviors.

This repeated activation of the basal ganglia also ultimately triggers changes in the way a person responds to stimuli associated with drinking alcohol, such as specific people, places, or alcohol-associated cues such as certain glassware or images or descriptions of drinking. Over time, these stimuli can trigger powerful urges to drink alcohol.

Repeated alcohol consumption also results in changes in the basal ganglia that lead to habit formation, ultimately contributing to compulsive use.

2. Negative Affect/Withdrawal Stage: reward deficits and stress surfeit

When a person who is addicted to alcohol stops drinking, they experience withdrawal symptoms—or symptoms that are opposite to the positive effects of alcohol that are experienced when drinking it. These symptoms can be physical (sleep disturbances, pain, feelings of illness) and emotional (dysphoria, irritability, anxiety, and emotional pain).

The negative feelings associated with alcohol withdrawal are thought to come from two sources. First, a diminished activation in the reward systems—or a reward deficit—of the basal ganglia makes it difficult for people to experience the pleasures of everyday living. Second, an increased activation of the brain's stress systems—or a stress surfeit—in the extended amygdala contributes to anxiety, irritability, and unease.

At this stage, the person no longer drinks alcohol for the pleasurable effects ("high"), but rather to escape the "low" feelings to which chronic alcohol misuse has contributed.

3. Preoccupation/Anticipation Stage: craving, impulsivity, and executive function

This is the stage at which an individual seeks alcohol again after a period of abstinence. A person becomes preoccupied with alcohol and how to get more of it, and looks forward to the next time he or she will consume it.

The prefrontal cortex—an area of the brain responsible for executive function, including the ability to organize thoughts and activities, prioritize tasks, manage time, and make decisions—is compromised in people experiencing alcohol addiction. As a result, this area of the brain plays a key role in this stage.

Hyperkatifeia

> "*Hyperkatifeia is a word that can be used to describe the negative emotional state associated with drug withdrawal. This overactive negative emotional state is hypothesized to drive the consumption of alcohol to find relief from this emotional state, and it may be caused by profound changes in the brain reward and stress systems.*"

Why Should We Be Concerned About AUD and Alcohol Addiction?

Alcohol consumption is linked to many health and social consequences, including interference with personal relationships, heart and liver diseases, cancers, motor vehicle collisions and other accidents, alcohol overdose, violence, homicide, and suicide. If a person has AUD, particularly if it is moderate to severe and involves alcohol addiction, they are more likely to regularly consume alcohol in levels associated with these effects on health.

Young people are especially at risk for AUD. Using alcohol during adolescence (from preteens to mid-20s) may affect brain development, making it more likely that they will be diagnosed with AUD later in life. However, most people with AUD—no matter their age or the severity of their alcohol problems—can benefit from treatment with behavioral health therapies, medications, or both.

How Common is Alcoholism? (The Statistics)

Alcohol use disorders are more common than may be imagined. Notes Psychology Today, studies have revealed that 29.1 percent of the US population (or 68.5 million) has experienced an alcohol use disorder (of varying grades) at some point in their lifetime. Within a 12-month period, approximately 13.9 percent (32.6 percent) of the US population experiences an alcohol use disorder. About 19.8 percent of the adults who have experienced an alcohol use disorder in their lifetime seek treatment or ask for help at some point.

As Psychology Today points out, about 75 percent of the alcohol that Americans drink occurs in the form of binge drinking. The symptoms of binge drinking include blackouts and memory lapses. Over time, a chronic binge drinker can develop serious liver damage and/or brain damage.

Physical and Psychological Symptoms of Alcohol Misuse & Dependence

Alcohol has immediate effects, as the American public clearly knows. The immediate impact of alcohol use on the body includes but is not limited to:

- Slowed reaction times
- Blackouts (again, usually in binge drinking episodes)
- Trouble with motor coordination or an inability to walk properly
- Impaired judgment and risk-taking without full consideration of the consequences (such as drunk driving)
- Memory impairment or memory lapses
- Slurred speech

An alcohol use disorder, especially at the more severe end of the spectrum, can lead to permanent and debilitating health conditions that may require care for a lifetime. Some of the most acute problems relate to the indirect problems that an alcohol use disorder causes.

A tipoff that a person's behavior has progressed to an alcohol use disorder concerns their nutritional habits. As alcohol misuse takes firmer root, people often neglect their nutritional health. The person may show signs of malnutrition, such as a gaunt appearance, hair loss or thinning, and dark circles under the eyes.

These may be symptoms of a general condition known as thiamine deficiency. The brain and all the tissue in the body need thiamine (B1) for healthy functioning. Individuals with an alcohol use disorder may be suffering from a thiamine deficiency, among other nutritional deficits.

The psychological effects of alcohol are immediately recognizable after a person drinks. Individuals may repeat themselves (due in part to memory lapse) and not show their familiar level of good judgment. Over time, individuals may develop sleep troubles and/ or mental health disorders such as depression or anxiety. Cognitive problems include a diminished attention span and problems with motor coordination, such as asterixis, a condition that causes a person to involuntarily flap or shake their hands. In severe cases, hepatic encephalopathy can develop and, for some, cause them to slip into a fatal hepatic coma.

If you believe you or someone you love is starting to show signs of alcohol misuse and need help or are unsure as to whether you can financially afford rehab, use our insurance verification tool below to see if all or part of the cost may be covered by your insurance provider.

Unfortunately, many people are unable to see the alcoholic symptoms within themselves and so the people around them must watch for the signs of an alcoholic. Alcoholic symptoms can typically be seen throughout the alcoholic's life such as at work, at school and with family. Those around the alcoholic may be reluctant to admit to the alcoholic signs and often make excuses for the alcoholic so they don't have to face the reality that their loved one is showing the symptoms of an alcoholic and likely has a problem.

Alcoholic Symptoms - Behavioral Signs of an Alcoholic

Behavioral signs of an alcohol addict can be some of the easiest to notice but unfortunately also may cause some of the most damage to those around the alcoholic. Behavioral signs of an alcoholic may

be seen by friends, family or even coworkers of the alcoholic.
Behavioral signs of an alcoholic include:

Has legal trouble such as DUI, domestic abuse or assault

Arrives for appointments, interviews, or meetings intoxicated, or misses them altogether

Frequently goes "on and off-the-wagon"

Behaves in an uncharacteristic, impulsive, or inappropriate manner

Is increasingly angry or defiant

Overreacts to ordinary circumstances and problems, advice and criticism

Is uncharacteristically isolated and withdrawn

Denies, lies, covers up or is secretive about behaviors and whereabouts

Loses interest in hobbies and activities

Takes unnecessary risks or acts in a reckless manner

Has increasing financial problems (may borrow or steal from family and friends)

Alcoholic Symptoms - Mental Signs of an Alcoholic

Mental signs of an alcoholic can be more difficult to spot and are often noticed by those who live with the alcoholic. Mental symptoms of an alcoholic often indicate a severe worsening of the disease and should not be ignored.
Mental alcoholic signs include:

Has difficulty concentrating, focusing, or attending to a task, needs help to complete a task

Frequently appears distracted or disoriented

Makes inappropriate or unreasonable choices

Has difficulty making decisions

Experiences short-term memory loss or blacks out

Often needs directions repeated

Has difficulty recalling known details

Is depressed or irritable

Alcoholic Symptoms - Physical Signs of an Alcoholic

Physical signs of an alcoholic are more difficult to pick up on then the behavioral signs of an alcoholic but once educated, alcoholic symptoms can be seen. Physical signs of an alcoholic are generally either caused by the drinking itself or by the withdrawal when the alcoholic is not drinking. (See physical effects of alcohol)
Physical symptoms of an alcoholic include:

Smell of alcohol on breath

Slurs speech or stutters, is incoherent, speaks slowly

Has difficulty maintaining eye contact

Has tremors (shaking or twitching of hands and eyelids)

Appears lethargic or falls asleep easily

Experiences sleep disturbances (e.g., insomnia, chronic fatigue)

Exhibits deteriorating personal hygiene, grooming, and posture

Exhibits impaired coordination or unsteady gait (e.g., staggering, off balance)

Has frequent injuries or bruises without reasonable explanations

Has chronic illnesses requiring doctors visits or hospitalization

Experiences wide mood swings (highs and lows)

Experiences general change in mood toward a more depressed and negative or critical outlook

Panic attacks

Alcoholic Symptoms - Signs of an Alcoholic on the Job

Just as alcoholic symptoms affect home and personal life, signs of an alcoholic are also seen on the job. Family members may not be made aware of job performance issues before it's too late, but co-workers who are friends of the alcoholic can notice the signs of an alcoholic and possibly turn to the family or alcoholic themselves. Signs of an alcoholic at work include:

Makes frequent performance mistakes

Gives questionable excuses or blames others for poor performance

Has difficulty adhering to schedules

Misses meetings and scheduled activities, is frequently late

Lodges numerous complaints or grievances

Uses excessive sick leave with poor excuses

Takes long lunch hours and breaks

Returns to work after breaks in a noticeably changed condition

Avoids supervisors and coworkers

Violates company policies and procedures

Behavioral Signs of Alcohol Misuse

As the National Council on Alcoholism and Drug Dependence explains, the behavioral signs of an alcohol use disorder will usually be apparent. People who experience alcohol misuse may become increasingly secretive about their activities because they may not want to hear people's concerns or get advice to stop. The individual may also drink in secret, either in a private place or out in public but away from concerned friends and family.

As a result of drinking, people may become more prone to accidents and show signs of injury, which they may try to cover up. An individual who is experiencing an alcohol use disorder may also hide alcohol around the house or at work. A person may become fearful of running out of alcohol, which in turn means that they keep a ready supply nearby.

Alcohol misuse can also lead people to show a diminished level of care for their hygiene and physical appearance. As alcohol misuse progresses, the individual may look increasingly as if they have not been showering, have stopped shaving, and are no longer washing or changing their clothes. Alcohol misuse often leads to problems in the person's relationships across the full spectrum of life. A person who has a rather calm affect when sober may shift into moodiness, depression, or irritability when intoxicated.

Additional behavioral signs of alcohol misuse include:

Increasing legal troubles, such as assault, domestic abuse, or drunk driving

Showing up intoxicated at work, a family function, or a meeting

Yo-yoing: drinking and then stopping in a repeated pattern over time

Overreacting to any perceived criticism levelled against their drinking

Experiencing increasing financial problems

Uncharacteristically taking loans, liquidating any assets, and depleting cash accounts

Stealing and likely lying about it

Engaging in risky activities, such as unprotected sex

Find Rehab for Alcoholism Near You

Take Our "Am I an Alcoholic?" Self-Assessment

Take our free, 5-minute "Am I an Alcoholic?" self-assessment below if you think you or someone you love might be struggling with an alcohol use disorder (AUD). The evaluation consists of 11 yes or no questions that are intended to be used as an informational tool to assess the severity and probability of an AUD. The test is free, confidential, and no personal information is needed to receive the result.

The Prevalence of Alcohol Misuse and Drunk Driving

One of the most troubling behavioral signs of an alcohol use disorder is drunk driving. The well-known nonprofit organization Mothers Against Drunk Driving publishes reliable statistics on drunk driving.

In 2013, 28.7 million Americans reported that they drove after drinking.

In 2014, 9,967 Americans died in car crashes that involved alcohol. This statistic translates to a fatal car crash every 53 minutes in the US. That's about 27 fatalities each day.

In 2014, about 290,000 Americans were injured in a car accident that involved drinking. This statistic translates to a car accident injury every two minutes.

On average, a person will drive drunk 80 times before being arrested for the first time.

If you or someone you know are showing signs of being drunk, do not let them get behind the wheel

How To Deal With Friends Who Drink If I Don't?

If you're the only one of your friends who doesn't drink alcohol, it can be a tough situation to handle. You may feel like you're on the outside looking in or that your friends don't really understand what you're going through.

On the other hand, if you do choose to drink, it can make you feel uncomfortable or guilty if they pressure you into drinking or make fun of you for not drinking. No matter which way you look at it, dealing with friends who drink if I don't is a real issue that many people face, especially if you are in recovery or struggling with your drinking.

Here, we will explore some effective strategies for dealing with this kind of problem and how to maintain healthy relationships with your friends while still staying true to yourself.

If You're The Only One Not Drinking, It Can Be Difficult To Deal With Friends Who Do

If you have friends who drink and you don't, it can be difficult to deal with them. You may feel left out or like you don't fit in. It's important to remember that you are not alone. There are many people who don't drink for a variety of reasons.

Here are a few tips to remember if your friends are drinking, but you're not. And remember— oftentimes the best solution is just to leave the situation entirely. If for some reason that can't happen:

•Remember: don't feel pressured to drink. Just because your friends are drinking doesn't mean you have to.

•If you're feeling uncomfortable, step away from the group for a bit. Go to the bathroom or get some fresh air.

•Stick to non-alcoholic drinks. There's no shame in ordering a soda or water instead of alcohol.

•Importantly, be honest with your friends about why you're not drinking. They may be more understanding than you think.

•If your friends don't understand, they might have the same problem as you. Try some sympathy— they may need help too.

Remember the dangers associated with alcohol and what you have overcome or are skipping entirely by not drinking. These dangers include:

•Drunk driving: Drunk driving is one of the most dangerous things that someone can do. If you have friends who drink, make sure they never get behind the wheel after drinking.

•Alcohol poisoning: Drinking too much alcohol can lead to alcohol poisoning, which can be deadly. If your friends are drinking heavily, make sure they are not alone and that someone knows how much they are consuming.

•Violence: Alcohol can make people more aggressive and violent. If you are around people who are drinking, be aware of this and stay out of any arguments or fights that may start.

•Unsafe sex: People who are drunk are more likely to engage in unsafe sex, which can lead to sexually transmitted diseases or unwanted pregnancies. If your friends are drinking, make sure they use protection if they plan on having sex.

How To Still Socialize With Friends Who Drink If You Don't

It can be tough to socialize and have fun without alcohol, but there are ways to deal with friends who drink if you don't. Here are some tips:

•Find other things to do together that don't involve drinking. You can still go out and have fun without alcohol. Suggest doing something else that you and your friends enjoy, like going to a movie or ice skating.

•Explain your reasons for not drinking to your friends. They may not understand why you don't drink, but if you explain it to them they may be more understanding. Let them know that you're still having fun even though you're not drinking.

•Don't judge your friends for drinking. Just because you don't drink doesn't mean you should judge those who do. Everyone is different and has their own reasons for drinking or not drinking.

•If you feel uncomfortable around your friends who are drinking, excuse yourself and leave the situation. You don't have to stay somewhere that makes you feel uncomfortable just because your friends are there.

How To Stay In Recovery While Others Are Drinking

If you're in recovery or simply don't drink alcohol, it can be tricky to deal with friends who do drink. Here are more tips on how to stay sober and in recovery while others are drinking:

•First and foremost, always put your sobriety first. Don't let peer pressure or social norms dictate your choices.

•Have a plan in place for what you'll do if you start to feel tempted to drink. This could involve calling a friend or family member, going for a walk, or anything that will help take your mind off of drinking.

•If you're feeling tempted, reach out to a sober friend or sponsor for support.

•Avoid potential triggers by hanging out in places that don't serve alcohol or by avoiding situations where you know there will be drinking (e.g., parties, bars).

•Keep yourself busy and distracted by engaging in other activities (e.g., talking to people, dancing, listening to music) instead of focusing on the drinking.

•Remember why you're choosing not to drink and what's important to you. This can help you stay motivated and focused on your goal of staying sober.

Get Help If You Just Can't Stay Sober

Dealing with friends who drink when you don't can be a challenge, but it doesn't have to be. By understanding that your choice is valid and communicating openly with your friends about why you choose not to drink, you can maintain healthy relationships while still staying true to yourself.

Remember, no matter what choices anyone else makes, the most important thing is that everyone respects each other's decisions and remains civil. If your friends can't, maybe they weren't really your friends in the first place. This can hurt, but staying sober is the most important thing— everything else follows..

When Is It Time for Treatment?

Alcohol-related problems—which result from drinking too much, too fast, or too often—are among the most significant public health issues in the United States.

Many people struggle with controlling their drinking at some time in their lives. More than 14 million adults ages 18 and older have alcohol use disorder (AUD), and 1 in 10 children live in a home with a parent who has a drinking problem.

Does Treatment Work?

The good news is that no matter how severe the problem may seem, most people with AUD can benefit from some form of treatment.

Research shows that about one-third of people who are treated for alcohol problems have no further symptoms 1 year later. Many others substantially reduce their drinking and report fewer alcohol-related problems.

Signs of an Alcohol Problem

Alcohol use disorder (AUD) is a medical condition that doctors diagnose when a patient's drinking causes distress or harm. The condition can range from mild to severe and is diagnosed when a patient answers "yes" to two or more of the following questions.

In the past year, have you:

• Had times when you ended up drinking more, or longer than you intended?

• More than once wanted to cut down or stop drinking, or tried to, but couldn't?

• Spent a lot of time drinking? Or being sick or getting over the aftereffects?

• Experienced craving—a strong need, or urge, to drink?

• Found that drinking—or being sick from drinking—often interfered with taking care of your home or family? Or caused job troubles? Or school problems?

• Continued to drink even though it was causing trouble with your family or friends?

• Given up or cut back on activities that were important or interesting to you, or gave you pleasure, in order to drink?

• More than once gotten into situations while or after drinking that increased your chances of getting hurt (such as driving, swimming, using machinery, walking in a dangerous area, or having unsafe sex)?

• Continued to drink even though it was making you feel depressed or anxious or adding to another health problem? Or after having had a memory blackout?

•Had to drink much more than you once did to get the effect you want? Or found that your usual number of drinks had much less effect than before?

•Found that when the effects of alcohol were wearing off, you had withdrawal symptoms, such as trouble sleeping, shakiness, irritability, anxiety, depression, restlessness, nausea, or sweating? Or sensed things that were not there?

If you have any of these symptoms, your drinking may already be a cause for concern. The more symptoms you have, the more urgent the need for change. A health professional can conduct a formal assessment of your symptoms to see if AUD is present. For an online assessment of your drinking pattern, go to RethinkingDrinking.niaaa.nih.gov.

Options for Treatment

When asked how alcohol problems are treated, people commonly think of 12-step programs or 28-day inpatient rehab but may have difficulty naming other options. In fact, there are a variety of treatment methods currently available, thanks to significant advances in the field over the past 60 years.
Ultimately, there is no one-size-fits-all solution, and what may work for one person may not be a good fit for someone else. Simply understanding the different options can be an important first step.

Types of Treatment

Behavioral Treatments

Behavioral treatments are aimed at changing drinking behavior through counseling. They are led by health professionals and supported by studies showing they can be beneficial.

Medications

Three medications are currently approved in the United States to help people stop or reduce their drinking and prevent relapse. They are prescribed by a primary care physician or other health professional and may be used alone or in combination with counseling.

Mutual-Support Groups

Alcoholics Anonymous (AA) and other 12-step programs provide peer support for people quitting or cutting back on their drinking. Combined with treatment led by health professionals, mutual-support groups can offer a valuable added layer of support.

Due to the anonymous nature of mutual-support groups, it is difficult for researchers to determine their success rates compared with those led by health professionals.

Starting With a Primary Care Doctor

For anyone thinking about treatment, talking to a primary care physician is an important first step—he or she can be a good source for treatment referrals and medications. A primary care physician can also:

Evaluate a patient's drinking pattern

Help craft a treatment plan

Evaluate overall health

Assess if medications for alcohol may be appropriate

Individuals are advised to talk to their doctors about the best form of primary treatment.

Types of Professionals Involved in Care

Many health professionals can play a role in treatment. Below is a list of providers and the type of care they may offer.

Provider Type	Degrees & Credentials	Treatment Type
Primary Care Provider	**M.D., D.O.** (Doctor of Osteopathic Medicine), additionally you may see a **Nurse Practitioner** or **Physician's Assistant**	Medications, Brief Behavioral Treatment, Referral to Specialist
Psychiatrist	M.D., D.O.	Medications, Behavioral Treatment
Psychologist	Ph.D., Psy.D., M.A.	Behavioral Treatment
Social Worker	**M.S.W.** (Master of Social Work), **L.C.S.W.** (Licensed Clinical Social Worker)	Behavioral Treatment
Alcohol Counselor	Varies—most States require some form of certification	Behavioral Treatment

Individuals are advised to talk to their doctors about the best form of primary treatment.

Treatments Led by Health Professionals

Professionally led treatments include:

Medications

Some are surprised to learn that there are medications on the market approved to treat alcohol dependence. The newer types of these medications work by offsetting changes in the brain caused by AUD.

All approved medications are non-addictive and can be used alone or in combination with other forms of treatment.

Behavioral Treatments

Also known as alcohol counseling, behavioral treatments involve working with a health professional to identify and help change the behaviors that lead to heavy drinking. Behavioral treatments share certain features, which can include:
- Developing the skills needed to stop or reduce drinking
- Helping to build a strong social support system
- Working to set reachable goals
- Coping with or avoiding the triggers that might cause relapse

Types of Behavioral Treatments

- Cognitive–Behavioral Therapy can take place one-on-one with a therapist or in small groups. This form of therapy is focused on identifying the feelings and situations (called "cues") that lead to heavy drinking and managing stress that can lead to relapse. The goal is to change the thought processes that lead to alcohol misuse and to develop the skills necessary to cope with everyday situations that might trigger problem drinking.
- Motivational Enhancement Therapy is conducted over a short period of time to build and strengthen motivation to change drinking behavior. The therapy focuses on identifying the pros and cons of seeking treatment, forming a plan for making changes in one's drinking, building confidence, and developing the skills needed to stick to the plan.
- Marital and Family Counseling incorporates spouses and other family members in the treatment process and can play an important role in repairing and improving family relationships.

Studies show that strong family support through family therapy increases the chances of maintaining abstinence (stopping drinking), compared with patients undergoing individual counseling.

•Brief Interventions are short, one-on-one or small-group counseling sessions that are time limited. The counselor provides information about the individual's drinking pattern and potential risks. After the client receives personalized feedback, the counselor will work with him or her to set goals and provide ideas for helping to make a change.

Ultimately, choosing to get treatment may be more important than the approach used, as long as the approach avoids heavy confrontation and incorporates empathy, motivational support, and a focus on changing drinking behavior.

What FDA-Approved Medications Are Available?

Certain medications have been shown to effectively help people stop or reduce their drinking and avoid relapse.

Current Medications

The U.S. Food and Drug Administration (FDA) has approved three medications for treating alcohol dependence, and others are being tested to determine whether they are effective.

Naltrexone can help people reduce heavy drinking.

Acamprosate makes it easier to maintain abstinence.

Disulfiram blocks the breakdown (metabolism) of alcohol by the body, causing unpleasant symptoms such as nausea and flushing of the skin. Those unpleasant effects can help some people avoid drinking while taking disulfiram.

It is important to remember that not all people will respond to medications, but for a subset of individuals, they can be an important tool in overcoming alcohol dependence.

Scientists are working to develop a larger menu of pharmaceutical treatments that could be tailored to individual needs. As more medications become available, people may be able to try multiple medications to find which they respond to best.

"Isn't taking medications just trading one addiction for another?" This is not an uncommon concern, but the short answer is "no." All medications approved for treating alcohol dependence are non-addictive. These medicines are designed to help manage a chronic disease, just as someone might take drugs to keep their asthma or diabetes in check.

Isn't taking medications just trading one addiction for another?"

This is not an uncommon concern, but the short answer is "no." All medications approved for treating alcohol dependence are non-addictive. These medicines are designed to help manage a chronic disease, just as someone might take drugs to keep their asthma or diabetes in check.

Looking Ahead: The Future of Treatment

Progress continues to be made as researchers seek out new and better treatments for alcohol problems. By studying the underlying causes of AUD in the brain and body, the National Institute on Alcohol Abuse and Alcoholism (NIAAA) is working to identify key cellular or molecular structures—called "targets"—that could lead to the development of new medications.

Personalized Medicine

Ideally, health professionals would be able to identify which AUD treatment is most effective for each person. NIAAA and other organizations are conducting research to identify genes and other factors that can predict how well someone will respond to a particular treatment. These advances could optimize how treatment decisions are made in the future.

Current NIAAA Research—Leading to Future Breakthroughs

Certain medications already approved for other uses have shown promise for treating alcohol dependence and problem drinking:

•The anti-smoking drug varenicline (marketed under the name Chantix) significantly reduced alcohol consumption and craving among people with AUD.

•Gabapentin, a medication used to treat pain conditions and epilepsy, was shown to increase abstinence and reduce heavy drinking. Those taking the medication also reported fewer alcohol cravings and improved mood and sleep.

•The anti-epileptic medication topiramate was shown to help people curb problem drinking, particularly among those with a certain genetic makeup that appears to be linked to the treatment's effectiveness.

Tips for Selecting Treatment

Professionals in the alcohol treatment field offer advice on what to consider when choosing a treatment program.

Overall, gather as much information as you can about the program or provider before making a decision on treatment. If you know someone who has first-hand knowledge of the program, it may help to ask about his or her personal experience.

Here are some questions you can ask that may help guide your choice:

What kind of treatment does the program or provider offer?
It is important to gauge whether the facility provides all the currently available methods or relies on one approach. You may want to learn if the program or provider offers medication and

if mental health issues are addressed together with addiction treatment.

Is treatment tailored to the individual?

Matching the right therapy to the individual is important to its success. No single treatment will benefit everyone. It may also be helpful to determine whether treatment will be adapted to meet changing needs as they arise.

What is expected of the patient?

You will want to understand what will be asked of you in order to decide what treatment best suits your needs.

Is treatment success measured?

By assessing whether and how the program or provider measures success, you may be able to better compare your options.

How does the program or provider handle relapse?

Relapse is common, and you will want to know how it is addressed. For more information on relapse, see Relapse Is Part of the Process.

When seeking professional help, it is important that you feel respected and understood and that you have a feeling of trust that this person, group, or organization can help you. Remember, though, that relationships with doctors, therapists, and other health professionals can take time to develop.

Additional Considerations

Treatment Setting—Inpatient or Outpatient?

In addition to choosing the type of treatment that's best for you, you'll also have to decide if that treatment is inpatient (you would stay at a facility) or outpatient (you stay in your home during treatment). Inpatient facilities tend to be more intensive and costly. Your healthcare provider can help you evaluate the pros and cons of each.

Cost may be a factor when selecting a treatment approach. Evaluate the coverage in your health insurance plan to determine how much of the costs your insurance will cover and how much you will have to pay. Ask different programs if they offer sliding scale fees—some programs may offer lower prices or payment plans for individuals without health insurance.

An Ongoing Process

Overcoming alcohol use disorder is an ongoing process, one which can include setbacks.

The Importance of Persistence

Because AUD can be a chronic relapsing disease, persistence is key. It is rare that someone would go to treatment once and then never drink again. More often, people must repeatedly try to quit or cut back, experience recurrences, learn from them, and then keep trying. For many, continued follow up with a treatment provider is critical to overcoming problem drinking.

Relapse Is Part of the Process

Relapse is common among people who overcome alcohol problems. People with drinking problems are most likely to relapse during periods of stress or when exposed to people or places associated with past drinking.

Just as some people with diabetes or asthma may have flare-ups of their disease, a relapse to drinking can be seen as a temporary setback to full recovery and not a complete failure. Seeking professional help can prevent relapse—behavioral therapies can help people develop skills to avoid and overcome triggers, such as stress, that might lead to drinking. Most people benefit from regular checkups with a treatment provider. Medications also can deter drinking during times when individuals may be at greater risk of relapse (e.g., divorce, death of a family member).

Mental Health Issues and Alcohol Use Disorder

Depression and anxiety often go hand in hand with heavy drinking. Studies show that people who are alcohol dependent are two to three times as likely to suffer from major depression or anxiety over their lifetime. When addressing drinking problems, it's important to also seek treatment for any accompanying medical and mental health issues.

Advice For Friends and Family Members

Caring for a person who has problems with alcohol can be very stressful. It is important that as you try to help your loved one, you find a way to take care of yourself as well. It may help to seek support from others, including friends, family, community, and support groups. If you are developing your own symptoms of depression or anxiety, think about seeking professional help for yourself. Remember that your loved one is ultimately responsible for managing his or her illness.

However, your participation can make a big difference. Based on clinical experience, many health providers believe that support from friends and family members is important in overcoming alcohol problems. But friends and family may feel unsure about how best to provide the support needed. The groups for family and friends listed below may be a good starting point.

Remember that changing deep habits is hard, takes time, and requires repeated efforts. We usually experience failures along the way, learn from them, and then keep going. AUD is no different. Try to be patient with your loved one. Overcoming this disorder is not easy or quick.

Pay attention to your loved one when he or she is doing better or simply making an effort. Too often we are so angry or discouraged that we take it for granted when things are going better. A word of appreciation or acknowledgement of a success can go a long way.

Professional help

Your doctor. Primary care and mental health practitioners can provide effective AUD treatment by combining new medications with brief counseling visits. To aid clinicians, NIAAA has developed a guide for younger patients, Alcohol Screening and Brief Intervention for Youth: A Practitioner's Guide. This guide and other resources are available at https://www.niaaa.nih.gov/health-professionals-communities.

Specialists in AUD. For specialty addiction treatment options, contact your doctor, health insurance plan, local health department, or employee assistance program. Other resources include:

National Institute on Alcohol Abuse and Alcoholism
www.niaaa.nih.gov
301–443–3860
National Institute on Drug Abuse
www.nida.nih.gov
301–443–1124
National Institute of Mental Health
www.nimh.nih.gov
1–866–615–6464

Research shows that most people who have alcohol problems are able to reduce their drinking or quit entirely.
There are many roads to getting better. What is important is finding yours.
Understanding the available treatment options—from behavioral therapies and medications to mutual-support groups—is the first step. The important thing is to remain engaged in whatever method you choose.
Ultimately, receiving treatment can improve your chances of success.

If your loved one needs help
Many people with alcohol use disorder hesitate to
get treatment because they don't recognize that
they have a problem. An intervention from loved
ones can help some people recognize and accept

that they need professional help. If you're concerned about someone who drinks too much, ask a professional experienced in alcohol treatment for advice on how to approach that person.

NINE

TABACCO AND NICOTINE ADDICTION

Tobacco is one of the most widely abused substances in the world. It is highly addictive. The Centers for Disease Control and Prevention estimates that tobacco causes 6 million deathsTrusted Source per year. This makes tobacco the leadingTrusted Source cause of preventable death.

Nicotine is the main addictive chemical in tobacco. It causes a rush of adrenaline when absorbed in the bloodstream or inhaled via cigarette smoke. Nicotine also triggers an increase in dopamine. This is sometimes referred to as the brain's "happy" chemical.

Dopamine stimulates the area of the brain associated with pleasure and reward. Like any other drug, use of tobacco over time can cause a physical and psychological addiction. This is also true for smokeless forms of tobacco, such as snuff and chewing tobacco.

What are the symptoms of tobacco and nicotine addiction?

A tobacco addiction is harder to hide than other addictions. This is largely because tobacco is legal, easily obtained, and can be consumed in public.

Some people can smoke socially or occasionally, but others become addicted. An addiction may be present if the person:

·cannot stop smoking or chewing, despite attempts to quit

·has withdrawal symptoms when they try to quit (shaky hands, sweating, irritability, or rapid heart rate)

·must smoke or chew after every meal or after long periods of time without using, such as after a movie or work meeting

·needs tobacco products to feel "normal" or turns to them during times of stress

·gives up activities or won't attend events where smoking or tobacco use is not allowed

·continues to smoke despite health problems

What are treatments for tobacco and nicotine addiction?

There are many treatments available for tobacco addiction. However, this addiction can be very difficult to manage. Many users find that even after nicotine cravings have passed, the ritual of smoking can lead to a relapse.

There are several different treatment options for those battling a tobacco addiction:

The patch

The patch is known as a nicotine replacement therapy (NRT). It's a small, bandage-like sticker that you apply to your arm or back. The patch delivers low levels of nicotine to the body. This helps gradually wean the body off it.

Nicotine gum

Another form of NRT, nicotine gum can help people who need the oral fixation of smoking or chewing. This is common, as people who are quitting smoking may have the urge to put something into their mouths. The gum also delivers small doses of nicotine to help the you manage cravings.

Spray or inhaler

Nicotine sprays and inhalers can help by giving low doses of nicotine without tobacco use. These are sold over the counter and are widely available. The spray is inhaled, sending nicotine into the lungs.

Medications

Some doctors recommend the use of medication to help with tobacco addictions. Certain antidepressants or high blood pressure drugs might be able to help manage cravings. One medication that's commonly used is varenicline (Chantix). Some doctors prescribe bupropion (Wellbutrin). This is an antidepressant that's used off-label for smoking cessation because it can decrease your desire to smoke.

Off-label drug use means that a drug that's been approved by the FDA for one purpose is used for a different purpose that has not been approved. However, a doctor can still use the drug for that purpose. This is because the FDA regulates the testing and approval of drugs, but not how doctors use drugs to treat their patients. So, your doctor can prescribe a drug however they think is best for your care.

Psychological and behavioral treatments

Some people who use tobacco have success with methods such as:
   ·hypnotherapy
   ·cognitive-behavioral therapy

•neuro-linguistic programming

These methods help the user change their thoughts about addiction. They work to alter feelings or behaviors your brain associates with tobacco use.

Treatment for a tobacco addition requires a combination of methods. Keep in mind that what works for one person won't necessarily work for another. You should talk to you doctor about what treatments you should try.

What is the outlook for tobacco and nicotine addiction?

Tobacco addiction can be managed with proper treatment. Addiction to tobacco is similar to other drug addictions in that it's never really cured. In other words, it is something that you will have to deal with for the rest of your life.

Tobacco users tend to have high relapse rates. It's estimated that about 75 percentTrusted Source of people who quit smoking relapse within the first six months. A longer treatment period or change in approach may prevent a future relapse.

Research has also shown that altering lifestyle habits, such as avoiding situations where there will be other tobacco users or implementing a positive behavior (like exercising) when cravings start can help improve chances for recovery.

A tobacco addiction can have fatal consequences without treatment. Tobacco use can cause:

•cancers of the lungs, throat, and mouth

•heart disease

•stroke

•chronic lung diseases such as emphysema and bronchitis

Any one of these conditions can be fatal. Quitting smoking or tobacco use can significantly reduce the risk of death due to these diseases. Even once the disease has been diagnosed, stopping tobacco use can improve treatment efforts.

Coping with Smoking Relapse

Quitting smoking can be one of life's most difficult challenges. You may need several attempts to finally reach your goal. The most common causes of relapse are stress, weight gain, and symptoms of nicotine and tobacco withdrawal.

The good news is that there are helpful ways of coping with smoking relapse. "Slips" may occur within the first week, months, or even years after you decide to quit smoking. While these unexpected urges may be dangerous, there are ways to cope with them.

I Slipped Up, Now What?

Most slipups occur within the first week of trying to quit smoking. Just because you take a puff or two of a cigarette or slide into a full-blown relapse doesn't mean that you can't begin again. The important thing to remember is that you're still in control and can move forward in your efforts to quit smoking.

Also, remember that you're not alone. Every year nearly 70 percentTrusted Source of all adult smokers report wanting to quit smoking completely. Millions of people try to quit smoking at least once during the year. Many people try a variety of methods to help them quit, including clinical interventions, counseling, nicotine replacement products, and alternative therapies.

A single slipup may result in negative feelings, depression, and self-condemnation. This can often lead to feelings of hopelessness and wanting to give up trying to quit. Several slips may result in a full-blown relapse, but it's never too late to start again. When you come face-to-face with the desire to smoke again, avoid thinking that just one cigarette won't hurt you. Instead, focus on the many health benefits you may enjoy from quitting smoking.

Relapse Triggers

Unexpected urges to smoke can be dangerous and cause you to relapse. Triggers, events, or circumstances can all work together to create a smoking relapse. It's important to make yourself aware of these triggers and avoid them, if at all possible.

Common relapse triggers may include:

•associating with other smokers, especially in a leisure environment

•consuming alcohol

•feeling overconfident

•becoming isolated from friends, family members, and support group members

•not getting enough sleep or rest

•encountering stressful situations on a frequent basis

•becoming a victim, with feelings of anger and self-pity

•adapting to a negative, pessimistic attitude

By eliminating as many triggers as possible, you can greatly increase your chance of quitting smoking successfully. While it may be impossible to eliminate all triggers, doing your best to prevent them ahead of time will provide you with a better likelihood of success.

Stress is one of the strongest smoking triggers, but also one that can be greatly reduced. Relieving stress can improve your quitting efforts both before and during a stressful situation. Learning to cope by using stress outlets can lead to success. Exercise, going for a walk, taking a warm bath, and meditation are all useful ways to eliminate stressful triggers in your life.

Surrounding yourself with a good network of supporters is helpful when coping with a smoking relapse or slipup. It's important to not get down on yourself and your failed attempts, but move forward and not give up.

Don't Give Up

Whether you've relapsed on one occasion or one hundred, you shouldn't give up your efforts to quit smoking. Most people try several times before succeeding. If you have relapsed, treat this incident as something to learn from, and an experience that you can use later on. Each and every attempt to quit smoking leads you that much closer to success.

Surrounding yourself with supporters can be encouraging during the quitting phase. Former smokers report that a good support network made up of family, friends, and co-workers is very helpful when trying to quit. If you don't have a large network of friends or family members at your disposal, your doctor and other health care professionals can offer support and encouragement.

ALL About NiCOTINE

Nicotine is a highly addictive chemical found in the tobacco plant. The addiction is physical, meaning habitual users come to crave the chemical, and also mental, meaning users consciously desire nicotine's effects. Nicotine addiction is also behavioral. People become dependent on actions involved with using tobacco. They also become accustomed to using tobacco in certain situations, such as after meals or when under stress.

Nicotine is primarily consumed by inhaling the smoke of tobacco cigarettes. Other ways to smoke tobacco include pipes and cigars. Smokeless tobacco is inhaled through the nose as a powder or held in the mouth.

Tobacco is dangerous. According to Study, smoking-related diseases are responsible for about 435,000 deaths per year in the United States. That's about 1 in every 5 deaths in the United States. Stopping smoking, no matter how long you have smoked, can greatly benefit your health.

The effects of nicotine addiction

Nicotine creates pleasant feelings in the body and mind. When you use tobacco, your brain releases neurotransmitters such dopamine, the feel-good chemical. This creates a brief feeling of contentment and pleasure.

But besides nicotine, tobacco cigarettes and smokeless tobacco contain many cancer-causing agents and other harmful chemicals. The nearly 4,000 chemicals found in tobacco have physical, mental, and psychological effects. Using tobacco leads to grave health complications, including:

- lung cancer
- emphysema
- chronic bronchitis
- cancer, especially in the respiratory system
- leukemia
- heart disease
- stroke
- diabetes
- eye issues, such as cataracts and macular degeneration
- infertility
- impotence
- miscarriage and pregnancy complications
- weakened immune system
- cold, flu, and respiratory infections
- loss of sense of taste or smell
- gum disease and dental issues
- the appearance of premature aging
- peptic ulcer disease
- osteoporosis

Secondhand smoke also increases the risk of lung cancer and heart disease among people close to smokers. According to the Centers for Disease Control and PreventionTrusted Source, children living in homes with secondhand smoke are more likely to have:

- sudden infant death syndrome
- asthma
- respiratory infections

·ear infections
·other illnesses

Causes of nicotine addiction

Smoking cigarettes or using other tobacco products causes nicotine addiction. Nicotine is very addictive, so even infrequent use can lead to dependence.

It's possible for smoking cessation products, such as nicotine gum, lozenges, or patches, to cause nicotine addiction. However, the risk is low. This is because the amount of nicotine in these products is lower and delivered more slowly than the nicotine in tobacco.

Who is at risk?

Anyone who uses tobacco is at risk of developing an addiction. The best way to prevent an addiction is to avoid tobacco.

Some factors may increase the risk of addiction. For example, people with a family history of nicotine addiction and people who grow up in homes with tobacco users are more likely to start smoking and develop an addiction.

Also, people who start smoking when they are young are more likely to smoke into adulthood. One studyTrusted Source notes that 80% of smokers began smoking by age 18 years. Starting smoking young tends to increase dependence later on in life. It's less common for adults to start smoking or develop an addiction, according to the American Society of Addiction Medicine.

People who abuse alcohol or drugs or who have a mental illness also have an increased risk of nicotine dependence.

Symptoms of nicotine addiction

Signs of nicotine addiction include:

·an inability to stop using tobacco products
    ·withdrawal symptoms when nicotine use stops
    ·a desire to keep smoking even when health complications arise
    ·continued use of tobacco products even if it negatively impacts your life

How it's diagnosed

To diagnose a nicotine addiction, your doctor will discuss your current usage and health history. He or she will determine the degree of your dependence and suggest treatment options.
People who want to seek treatment for addiction will need to commit to stopping.

How it's treated

The physical part of the addiction can be challenging to deal with. To be successful, the person must work to change behaviors and routines. There are many treatment options for nicotine addiction, including prescription medication, nicotine replacement therapy, and support groups.

Medications

Some medications can help you quit smoking. They work to lessen cravings. One option is nicotine replacement therapy via patches, gums, lozenges, nasal sprays, or inhalers. These options provide nicotine without the other chemicals found in tobacco. They allow you to defeat the addiction in a slow and methodical manner.
Non-nicotine options include antidepressants. These work to increase dopamine production to improve your mood.

Support groups

Whether you choose an in-person support group or a virtual one, support groups can teach you coping skills, help you work through your addiction, and offer you fellowship with other people facing the same challenges as you.

Home care

Treatment for nicotine addiction focuses largely on medications and taking the time to work through withdrawal symptoms and learn coping skills. Try these suggestions to make your transition away from nicotine easier:
·Get regular exercise.
·Choose snacks that keep your mouth and hands busy.
·Remove all tobacco products from your home and car.
·Avoid situations that could trigger a relapse, including being around other smokers.
·Choose healthy meals.
·Set realistic expectations about your treatment.
·Set small goals and reward yourself for meeting those goals.
Alternative and natural remedies

Other solutions that can help you overcome your addiction include:

·hypnosis
·acupuncture
·herbs
·essential oils
However, the safety and efficacy of each option is mostly unknown.

Effects of nicotine withdrawal

Addicted tobacco users who stop using nicotine products will face withdrawal. Effects of nicotine withdrawal include irritability, anxiety, and physical symptoms, such as headaches and fatigue. The first week will be the worst for withdrawal symptoms, but each passing day will get easier. Even when withdrawal symptoms have subsided, though, sudden cravings are common. Learning discipline is vital for these situations.

Managing Nicotine Withdrawal

No matter how you do it, you will likely encounter withdrawal symptoms at some point in your quit smoking journey. You do not have to give in to these symptoms and give up your quest to be smoke-free. Here are a few tips for coping with your withdrawal symptoms.

Exercise Nicotine can improve mood and may give you a false sense of well-being. Without the drug, you may begin to feel slightly depressed. Thirty minutes of exercise each day can help beat the sagging feeling of fatigue and depression by boosting natural "feel-good" endorphins in your body. Exercise may also help you sleep better. For best results, avoid exercising right before you go to bed. Give yourself three to four hours of downtime before you go to bed.

Sleep and Rest Your body is going through a lot of change as it works to rid itself of the nicotine dependence. It's normal to feel extra tired while you are going through nicotine withdrawal. Take naps, or go to bed earlier. Your body still detoxes while you're asleep.

Distract Yourself Sometimes people gain weight when they are trying to quit smoking, because they try to satisfy their cravings for a cigarette with food. This is another reason people put off quitting — fear of gaining weight. Find a distraction other than food when you begin craving a cigarette. You might try playing a game, reading your favorite website, or going for a walk. The goal is to get yourself away from the temptation and busy focusing on a different idea.

Make Your Life Smoke-Free Ask friends and family members to respect your new lifestyle and refrain from smoking around you.

This may mean asking them to smoke only outside, and not in your house or car.

Manage Stress In the past, you turned to cigarettes as a quick pick-me-up when times were stressful — but no more. Now you have to find techniques to deal with everyday stress in a healthier way. Physical activity, such as walking, cleaning the house, or gardening can help you reduce your stress while keeping your mind off of nicotine cravings. Deep breathing techniques or meditation can help you find calm and avoid taking stress out in less constructive ways. Whatever way you find works best for you, remember to turn to that when you need to let off some steam.

Turn to Your Accountability Partner Be honest, and tell them about your withdrawal. Let them know the rationalizations you're making: "Just one cigarette won't set me back too much" or "I'll smoke a cigarette just this once to get through this craving."
Your partner can help you identify ways you are sabotaging your quit-smoking plan, and can provide the support and encouragement to get through the craving.

Outlook for nicotine addiction

People who use nicotine products are at a greatly increased risk of respiratory diseases, cancers (especially lung cancer), stroke, and heart disease. Regardless of how long you've smoked, you can minimize your risk of health problems by stopping.

Overcoming nicotine withdrawal is often the most difficult part of quitting smoking. Many people have to try more than once to quit. The more you try to quit, the more likely you'll succeed.
There are many situations in your daily life that may trigger your desire to smoke. These situations can intensify symptoms of nicotine withdrawal. Triggers include:
- being around other smokers
- being in a car
- feeling stressed
- drinking coffee or tea

- drinking alcohol
- feeling bored
- talking on the phone

Identify your triggers, and try to avoid them if you can. In general, the symptoms of nicotine withdrawal pass quickly. Most symptoms pass within a week.

Once the symptoms of withdrawal stop, you may still experience long-term cravings for tobacco. Curbing these cravings will be important for long-term success.

Many people can manage cravings by avoiding triggers, engaging in moderate physical activity, and practicing deep breathing exercises. Finding ways to relax can curb cravings as well, such as:

- Listen to music.
- Participate in a hobby.
- Take a walk.
- Talk with friends and family.

Another helpful tip is to substitute carrots, gum, or hard candy for cigarettes. These can curb the psychological need to smoke.

TEN

DOES SOCIETY HAVE A SEX AND PORN ADDICTION PROBLEM?

Is Porn Addiction the Same as Sex Addiction?

Porn addiction and sex addiction are not the same disorder. Addiction to porn is considered to be a type of sex addiction and can manifest itself differently than other types of sex addiction. Like "sex addiction," "porn addiction" is not an official diagnosis in the DSM-5 yet. However, an addiction to porn can lead to serious distress and consequences in many facets of life.

Porn addiction, which is a subset of sex addiction, can refer to a range of behaviors that are done in excess and negatively impact one's life. "Porn addiction" is not an official diagnosis in the Diagnostic and Statistical Manual of Mental Disorders-V (DSM-5). However, an addiction to porn can lead to serious consequences in many aspects of one's life.

Pornography Statistics

40 million adults in the U.S. visit internet pornography sites on a regular basis.

1 in 5 internet searches on a mobile device are for pornography.

Men who are happily married are 61% less likely to look at porn.

20% of men admit to viewing pornography at work.

88% of porn scenes contain physical aggression. 49% contain verbal aggression.

Signs and Symptoms of Porn Addiction

•Excessive viewing of pornography.

•The definition of "excessive" depends on what you consider healthy, or it is the point at which pornography starts to have a negative impact on some aspect of your (or someone else's) life.

•Watching pornography interferes with normal daily behavior or responsibilities.

•More time spent watching pornography, or searching for more stimulating types of pornography, is needed to get you aroused or to climax, i.e., you develop a tolerance.

•There is a sense of emotional distress, or feeling of withdrawal, when porn use is stopped.

•Continued use pornography despite serious consequences (e.g., loss of relationship or job, contraction of a sexually transmitted disease or "STD").

•Compulsive masturbating.

•Sexual dysfunction (e.g., impotence, premature ejaculation).

•Use of pornography negatively affects your relationships, for example:

•It is more difficult to become aroused by your partner.

•Romantic or sexual behavior between you and your partner changes (e.g., becomes more aggressive, dominant, or emotionally disconnected).

•You watch porn as a way to alter your mood (e.g., obtain a "high") or avoid other unpleasant feelings, like anxiety or depression.

It is always recommended to speak with a healthcare professional if you are seriously concerned about your behavior. A healthcare professional will be best suited to help you understand your behaviors and treatment options.

What Causes Porn Addiction?

Porn addiction, like other substances or "things" that people can become addicted to, can be understood through principles of "operant conditioning."

This is where a certain behavior, watching porn in this case, is "reinforced," or rewarded, which in turn makes you want to do it again (and again).

Lots of different things can be reinforcing, and thus influence our behavior, but porn can be especially reinforcing because the reward taps into a very basic instinctual drive–sex. Therefore, it is very easy to become addicted to porn–it is accessing a fundamental (and very enjoyable) natural drive. It is also much easier to obtain than going out and finding a "mate" to fulfill this drive.

The problem occurs when seeking sexual pleasure becomes excessive, impulsive, or comes at the expense of other valued behaviors. Then we might say that one has a porn addiction.

Other Factors Influencing Porn Addiction

Biological

·You may have a genetic predisposition to impulsivity, emotion dysregulation, or sensation-seeking behavior.

·You may have a predisposition to other characteristics that are associated with sexual addiction, like anxiety or depression.

·As you might expect, higher levels of sex hormones like testosterone or estrogen can affect libido.

·If you are inclined towards impulsive behavior and have high levels of sex-related hormones, you may be more likely to engage in excessive or compulsive porn watching.

Psychological

·Early-life environmental factors, including adverse events like abuse or exposure to sexual content, can contribute to some of the underlying traits involved in porn addiction behaviors.

·Mental health:

·Anxiety.

·Depression.

·Personality disorders.

·Poor impulse control.

·Performance anxiety.

·Other mental health issues might contribute to porn addiction behaviors.

Social

·Rejection in relationships and social circles can lead to other, less healthy ways to find sexual gratification.

·Social isolation:

Not only does social isolation increase one's likelihood of seeking inappropriate ways of being sexually gratified, it also leads to a host of other problems—like depression and physical maladies—that can contribute to porn addictions or unhealthy sex behaviors.

·Peer influence:

If others around you are doing something, you are more likely to do it, too. Having a friend, or a group of friends, for example, who engage in excessive porn viewing can influence your behavior.

Effects of Addiction to Pornography

PHYSICAL

·Sexual dysfunction.
    ·Impotence (inability to form or maintain an erection).
    ·Premature ejaculation.

PSYCOLOGICAL

·Preoccupation with sexual thoughts throughout the day.
    ·Guilt, shame, confusion.
    ·Ambivalence about stopping, or cycles of stopping/restarting.
    ·Tendency towards other impulsive behaviors.
    ·Depression, anxiety, or other co-occurring psychological disorders.

SOCIAL

·Not wanting to seek person-to-person (real life) sexual contact, or diminished patience for sexual contact (e.g., wanting to have sex right away, or fantasizing or obsessing about sexual contact with random strangers).
    ·Decline in romantic or sexual interactions with partner, such as:
    ·Inability to become aroused.
    ·Increasing need for more aggression or dominance.
    ·Emotional detachment.

Porn Addiction in Teenagers

Due to the accessibility of sexually explicit material on the internet, porn addiction is becoming a growing concern in teenagers. With the click of a button they can be exposed to endless pages of adult content.

Porn Statistics in Teens

·9/10 boys are exposed to some form of pornography before the age of 18.

·6/10 girls are exposed to pornography before 18 years old.

·On average, a male's first exposure to pornography is at 12 years old.

·71% of teens have done something to hide what they do online from their parents.

·Teenage boys, 12-17 years old, have the highest risk of developing a porn addiction.

Viewing pornography can have negative consequences on teenagers down the line, affecting both their psychological and physical wellbeing. These ramifications include:

·Increase in high-risk behaviors.

·Skewed view of the world.

·Decrease in ability to build healthy relationships.

·Normalization of sexual violence.

·Increase in aggression towards women.

Research reveals that teenagers exposed to sexually explicit websites are more likely to be promiscuous and more likely to have used alcohol or other intoxicating substances during their last sexual encounter. This puts them at a higher risk for developing a substance abuse disorder or mental health disorder.

Can Porn Addiction Be Treated?

Yes. Porn addiction, like other addictions and mental health issues, can be treated through a number of different approaches.

Individual/Group Therapy

Individual or group therapy with a qualified mental health professional is always a safe approach. Individual therapy will usually consist of 30-60 minute sessions, focusing on your behaviors related to porn addiction and any related issues.

Group therapy will allow you to be in a community of others who are struggling with a similar experience.

Cognitive-Based Therapy (CBT)

CBT is based on the concept that our thoughts, emotions, and behaviors are all related, and when these become "dysfunctional" or overwhelmingly negative, it leads to serious consequences in our lives.

CBT will often focus on negative thoughts about oneself, others, and the world (e.g., "I will never stop watching porn") and work to change these into more positive, or functional, thoughts (e.g., "If I work at it, I will be able to stop watching porn").

Structured assignments and careful self-observation will guide individuals on the path to recovering.

Motivational Interviewing (MI)

An MI approach will work on "meeting you where you are at" in your current addiction and help you make your own decision when, and if, you are ready to make a change in your life.

MI is a less confrontational approach between the therapist and patient, but it can have a powerful, dramatic, and long-lasting effect on one's behavior.

Mindfulness-Based Therapies

Mindfulness-Based Therapies incorporate "mindfulness" as a key ingredient in treatment. Mindfulness is the cultivation of attention that is present-focused and nonjudgmental.

Mindfulness-based approaches help individuals gain more awareness over their thoughts, emotions, bodily sensations, and behaviors, and help them "relate" to these experiences in a different way. This allows these "temporary" and "fleeting" experiences to rise and pass away instead of letting them control one's behavior.Examples of mindfulness-based therapies include:

·Mindfulness-Based Stress Reduction (MBSR).
·Dialectical Behavioral Therapy (DBT).
·Acceptance and Commitment Therapy (ACT).
·Compassion-based practices, like Compassion-Focused Therapy, are related to mindfulness-based approaches.

Psychodynamic Therapy

Psychodynamic therapy works under the assumption that unconscious drives, conflicts, and memories are influencing our behavior. This therapy will traditionally explore early-childhood life events and their contribution to creating habits or "patterns" in one's life; however, it can also be present-focused and help the patient identify what is currently keeping them "stuck" in a certain behavior, in this case porn addiction.

Couples Therapy/Counseling

Couple's counseling can be very important for partners when one, or both, individuals watch porn in an unhealthy way. This type of counseling will focus on both resolving individual addictions or behaviors, and improving communication, relations, and healthy sexual functioning between the two partners.

Medications for Porn Addiction

The FDA has not approved any medication solely for the purpose of treating porn addiction. Some research of different medications has revealed promising results in decreasing the symptoms of porn addiction but there is a lack of randomized, controlled trials.

Porn addiction and related sexual dysfunctions oftentimes co-occur with mental health disorders such as depression and anxiety. These mental health issues can be treated using antidepressants (such as Selective Serotonin Reuptake Inhibitors or "SSRIs") or related drugs, which can reduce sexual cravings associated with porn addiction.

If a patient doesn't respond well to antidepressants or experiences unpleasant side effects, there are a couple alternatives:

·Naltrexone, a medication typically used to ease withdrawal symptoms in alcoholics and opioid addicts, has shown a decrease in sexual compulsions.

·Anti-androgenic medications can help to decrease sexual urges by reducing the amount of male hormones present in the body.

·There is not an adequate amount of research concerning anti-androgenic medications and severe side effects have been revealed.

·The effects of anti-androgenic medications lack permanence; hormone levels will return to normal once the drug is no longer taken.

These medications have only been used to treat those with paraphilia (a condition in which a person is sexually aroused by atypical or abnormal behaviors).

Although some research has been conducted, conclusive recommendations cannot be made due to a lack of reliable evidence.

Mental Health Disorders

Evidence reveals a high correlation between porn addiction and psychiatric conditions, specifically mood, anxiety, and personality disorders.

Studies have indicated that pornography viewers have higher levels of depressive symptoms and a poorer quality of life. This explains why antidepressants can be effective in treating porn addiction.

Clinical depression, which porn addicts commonly suffer from, is a severe mental health illness that requires professional treatment. Typical symptoms include:

·Suicidal thoughts or attempts.

·Irritability.

·Restlessness.

·Feelings of guilt or worthlessness.

·Fatigue

·Inability to concentrate.

·Sleeping too little or too much.

·Loss of interest in hobbies and activities that were once enjoyable.

·Continuous sad, anxious, or empty mood.

If you are addicted to porn and think you suffer from clinical depression, contact your medical provider immediately. It is vital that your treatment plan addresses both your depression and sex addiction.

Substance Abuse

Research indicates that the*use of pornography* can cause sexually compulsive and dependent behaviors, which **can lead to the development of a sex addiction** as well,. There is also a significant **correlationbetween sexual addiction and substance use disorders**.

.According to some research, an estimated 40-64% of sex addicts also have a substance abuse disorder.

.Alcohol abuse is most common, present in 30-40%, followed by marijuana abuse, present in 18-21.7%.

Furthermore, teenagers who view sexually explicit material are more likely to have used alcohol or other illicit substances during their most recent sexual encounter. The earlier someone begins using a substance, the more likely it is that he or she will become addicted. Therefore, teens who develop a porn addiction are at a greater risk for developing a substance abuse disorder as well.

One study has revealed that frequent use of pornography by boys aged 18 years old has been associated with co-occurring problematic behaviors such as consuming alcohol more often and selling sex.

Treating co-occurring addictions is a complex process. Medical professionals must assess the pattern of drug use and pornography viewing and how they relate to each other. Once the interaction of both addictions is assessed, then appropriate treatment can be administered.

If you think that you have issues with both porn addiction and substance addiction, it is critical to your recovery that you find a treatment center that can cater specifically to your needs. Call today.

Is My Child is Addicted to Porn?

There is no official medical definition of pornography addiction but there is extensive medical literature focused on the topic. That being said, there are some behavioral signs that often co-occur with excessive porn use:

·ADHD symptoms:
·Impaired concentration.
·Easily distracted.
·Struggle to follow instructions.
·Does not seem to listen when spoken to.
·Anxiousness:
·Mental distress or unease.
·Withdrawn or isolated.
·Anger and impatience.
·Seems depressed.
·Avoids previously enjoyed pursuits.

Additionally, there are some signs associated with computer use that a parent should be aware of when evaluating for porn addiction:

·Your child spends large amounts of time online (especially at night).

·Your child turns off the computer or quickly changes the screen when you enter the room.

·Your child locks the door while on the computer.
·Your child lies about computer use.
·Your child erases his or her search history.
·You find pornographic pictures on the computer.

What Should I Do if My Child is Addicted to Porn?

Due to the increased accessibility of porn on the internet, children and teens are at a higher risk for developing an addiction to porn than in the past. Porn addiction is especially traumatizing for children and teens, as their brains are still developing. It can cause emotional disturbances and mental health issues if left untreated.

If you suspect that your child is addicted to porn, you may want to approach them in a calm and nonjudgmental fashion. You can begin by asking your child the following questions:

·Have you ever viewed internet pornography? If so, when did you begin viewing it?

·How often do you watch it and for how long?

·Why do you watch internet pornography/

·When was the last time you viewed internet pornography?

It's extremely important to maintain open communication and to make sure your child feels comfortable talking to you about his or her addiction. This will ensure a positive healing environment for your child or teen.

If you are worried about a sudden change in your child's behavior and suspect that it is related to porn use, there is hope for recovery. Call to speak to a treatment support specialist and learn about treatment options for your child.

Porn Addiction Treatment Options for Teens

Although the Diagnostic and Statistical Manual of Mental Disorders-V (DSM-5) does not list porn addiction as a diagnosable condition yet, there are a few treatment options that cater specifically to teenagers suffering from a porn addiction.

·**Outpatient therapy:** Extensive therapy in which the teen can still live at home, attend school, and participate in any other activities.

·**Residential treatment centers**: Overnight facilities in which the teen can escape his or her everyday, sexualized habits and focus on developing more positive behaviors.

·**Peer support groups:** Teen-focused support groups create a safe and healing environment in which the teen can express him or herself openly.

How to Help Prevent Your Child From Developing a Porn Addiction

As a parent, it is crucial to have open communication with your child. It is not recommended that you avoid the topic of sex, as your child may have many questions pertaining to sexual relationships and development. There are some important factors to consider when attempting to prevent your child from developing a porn addiction:

·Maintain a communicative and honest parent-child relationship.

·Provide sex education and guide them to appropriate resources.

·Utilize parental controls and carefully monitor internet use.

·Lead by example and limit your own technology usage.

> " *so you may have to fight a battle more than once to win it......* "

Sexua Addiction

Sex addiction is the compulsive engagement in sexual acts despite negative consequences. Moreover, it is emotionally distressing rather than fulfilling.

The concept of sex addiction has been thought of in a variety of ways. Thus, it is often referred to by several different names. Hypersexuality, hypersexual disorder, sexual compulsivity, sexual impulsivity, and sexual addiction disorder are all names used when referring to sexual addiction. While not always recognized as a legitimate diagnosis, sex addiction does have real consequences.

This addiction can have a negative impact on a person's relationships, occupation, mental well-being, and more.

> *"Sex addiction can refer to a range of behaviors that are done in excess and significantly impact one's life in a negative way.*
>
> *The Diagnostic and Statistical Manual of Mental Disorders-V (DSM-5) does not list sex addiction as a diagnosable condition yet, but research indicates that there is a clear prevalence of adverse sexual behavior that is similar in development to a "chemical" addiction."*

Is a sex addiction similar to other addictions?

Yes. The "addiction feeling" is what makes it similar. The craving for sex is similar to cravings felt for alcohol or drugs by those who have addictions to these substances. It's an overwhelming compulsion or temptation that's so strong you feel that you have to have it. It's an out-of-control feeling, never feeling satisfied feeling or a constant battle to take control of something that's on autopilot. You return to the behavior — over and over again — despite the negative consequences.

How common is sexual addiction and who is most affected?

Hypersexuality appears to affect about 3% to 10% of the general U.S. population. It's more common in men than women. For every two to five males with hypersexuality, one woman is affected. Sexual addiction begins, on average, at 18 years of age. Most individuals don't reach out for professional help until age 37.

Many individuals (88%) have a history of other mental health conditions, too, including:

Mood disorders, including bipolar disorder.

Anxiety disorders.

History of suicide attempts.
Personality disorders.
Other addictive disorders.
Impulse control disorders.
Obsessive-compulsive disorder (OCD).
Attention deficit hyperactivity disorder (ADHD).

Is sex addiction or hypersexuality considered a mental health disorder?

Debate is ongoing if hypersexuality can be classified as a mental health disorder. The American Psychiatric Association rejected a proposal to include hypersexual disorder as a condition in DSM-5 (Diagnostic and Statistical Manual of Mental Disorders, fifth edition), their manual for assessing and diagnosing mental health conditions. Their reason was lack of evidence and the potential consequences of calling excessive sexual activity a "pathology" (calling it a disease or disorder).

What does a sexual addict think or feel about their sexual obsession?

A sex addict may feel:
- Guilt, shame or remorse.
- Hopelessness, powerless over the addictive behavior.
- Depressed, lonely.
- Fearful, anxious.
- Suicidal.

What are the signs and symptoms of sexual addiction or hypersexuality?

Although there's no established criteria for hypersexuality, traits that are commonly seen in a hypersexual person or sexual addict include:

•**You're obsessed with sex**. You spend a lot of time fantasizing about your sexual urges and engaging in sexual behavior.

•**You masturbate often** (once to several times daily).

•**You frequently view pornography.** Sources include videos, adult magazines, the internet (websites, webcams). You often masturbate while viewing pornography.

•**You spend an excessive amount of time planning sexual activity.** You spend a lot of time figuring out where and how you'll get your next sexual "high."

•**You frequently use sexual services.** This is a step up, in that your activities now involve human interaction. Behaviors could include phone sex, connections made through internet chat rooms, paying for sexual encounters, visits to strip clubs, having multiple partners or frequent one-night stands.

•**Your behavior escalates to reckless sexual activity.** You may add substance abuse to your sexual activity or add sexual aggression or dangerous sexual activity (such as autoerotic asphyxiation) to your behaviors.

•**You engage in sexual behaviors that go against your personal values**, religious beliefs or what society deems appropriate.

•**You frequently engage in paraphilia.** These are sexual behaviors that involve another person's psychological distress, injury or death. Examples include exhibitionism (exposing genitals to strangers), voyeurism (watching or engaging in sexual activities with others), sadomasochism (sexual pleasure from inflicting pain or humiliation on others) and pedophilia (sexual feelings toward children).

•**You can't stop your sexual behavio**r despite negative consequences to your finances, relationships, health or emotions.

What are the complications of having a sexual addition or hypersexuality?

Complications of sexual addiction include:

·Lack of a normal, healthy relationship with your sexual partner and your family.

·Downward work performance and career loss from an inability to focus on work or watching pornography at work.

·Money problems stemming from paying for sexual activities.

·Health consequences, including pregnancy and sexually transmitted infections (STIs), such as HIV, hepatitis B and C, syphilis or gonorrhea.

·Use of recreational drugs or drinking an excessive amount of alcohol.

·Development of mental health conditions, such as stress and anxiety, depression or thoughts of suicide.

·Potential jail or prison time for sexual offenses.

·Emotional costs including guilt, shame and hopelessness.

What causes sexual addiction or hypersexuality?

Scientists aren't totally sure what causes hypersexuality. Possible theories include:

·**Imbalance of mood chemicals in your brain.** High levels or overactivity of certain chemicals in your brain called neurotransmitters (dopamine, norepinephrine and serotonin) might result in increased sexual desire and behavior.

·**Conditions that affect or damage areas of your brain that control sexual behavior.** Conditions such as dementia, epilepsy, bipolar disorder and damage to your frontal lobe, amygdala or prefrontal cortex areas of your brain may contribute to hypersexuality.

·**Altered brain function** that creates new nerve pathways of addictive behavior.

·**Substance abuse,** particularly cocaine and amphetamine use and alcohol.

·**Adverse effect of medication.** One example is levodopa, a common medication used in Parkinson's disease.

How is hypersexuality diagnosed?

Your healthcare professional or mental health professional may ask you about your:

·Current health, existing health conditions, family medical history, current medications, supplements and herbal products.

·Use of recreational drugs and alcohol.

·Sexual thoughts, urges and behaviors, and level of control you feel you have over them, as well as other sexual symptoms (see Symptoms and Causes section).

Your healthcare provider may ask for your permission to talk with your family and friends to gain more input.

Your healthcare provider may also want to rule out other conditions for which hypersexuality may be a symptom, such as bipolar disorder (manic episode), hyperandrogenism, anxiety, personality disorder, obsessive-compulsive disorder and Tourette's disorder.

At present, there isn't an agreed diagnostic criteria for hypersexuality. Despite this, mental health professionals skilled in addiction disorders will recognize life-consuming sexual behaviors and can offer appropriate treatment options.

How is sexual addiction, hypersexuality, treated?

Sexual addiction, or hypersexuality, is treated with a combination of medications, psychotherapy and self-help group therapy.

Medications

No medication is specifically approved to treat sexual addiction. However, medications that act on your brain's "urge and behavior" hormones and chemicals and that are prescribed for similar medical conditions can be tried. Your healthcare provider will prescribe medications that are best suited for you, considering any other mental health conditions you may have.

·**Antidepressants**. Selective serotonin reuptake inhibitors (SSRIs) are considered first-line treatment for sexual addiction.

·**Anti-androgens**. These medications target male sex hormones. They're useful in reducing obsessive thoughts. They might be tried in extreme cases of sexual acting out, when behaviors are dangerous to others.

·**Naltrexone (Vivitrol®, Revia®)**. This drug, used to treat alcohol and opioid addiction, has been shown to be helpful in treating gambling addiction and may be helpful for sex addiction.

·**Mood stabilizers**. These drugs may be useful if you have bipolar disorder with manic or impulsive features and when hypersexuality is a feature. Some examples include lithium, valproate (Depakote®) and carbamazepine (Tegretol®).

·**Anti-anxiety medications**. These drugs may be tried if sexual behavior is triggered by anxiety. Buspirone is one example that may be helpful.

·**Other medications**. Antipsychotics may be considered when thought disorders or severe agitation are prominent features. These medications can reduce sexual desire, arousal and orgasm. If you have attention deficit hyperactivity disorder (which is linked to sexual risk taking), methylphenidate and dextroamphetamine may be a useful choice.

Psychotherapy

Psychotherapy involves a variety of techniques. During psychotherapy, you'll talk with a mental health professional who'll help you identify and manage factors that might be triggering your hypersexuality behaviors. Psychotherapy is provided to individuals, as well as to families and couples, since all are affected by an individual's sexual addiction.

·**Cognitive behavioral therapy**. This type of psychotherapy focuses on replacing negative thoughts and behaviors with other ways to better cope and reduce the impulse to have sex.

·Acceptance and commitment therapy. This psychotherapy uses acceptance and mindfulness strategies. Its goal is for individuals to accept distress and to change the relationship with their thoughts rather than changing the thoughts themselves.

·Motivational interviewing. This psychotherapy guides individuals through the process of exploring their sexual addiction in the context of your personal goals and values.

Can sexual addiction or hypersexuality be prevented?

Whether or not sexual addiction can be prevented depends on the underlying cause(s). Sometimes, there's a chemical imbalance in your brain. Or, another health condition's side effect or symptom is hypersexuality. There are many factors that come into play in the development or appearance of a sexual addiction.

But even if you can't control all the factors, you can take some control of some things that might escalate your thoughts, urges, desires and actions. These include:

·Learn about sexual addiction or hypersexuality. You're taking your first step now by reading this article! See your healthcare professional or mental healthcare professional. They're here to help you, beginning with education.

·Change triggers that you know tempt you. Block pornography internet sites and other sex sites on your computer. Drive a different route to avoid strip clubs. Think about other changes you can make.

·Get help for substance abuse problems. If you abuse alcohol or recreational drugs, you reduce your chance of resisting your sexual urges. Ask your healthcare provider for help in quitting these substances.

·Make sure other mental health conditions are well managed. If you have other mental health conditions, such as depression, anxiety or bipolar disorder, make sure you're following all of your doctor's instructions for managing these conditions. If you think your condition has changed, make an appointment and see your healthcare provider.

·**Channel your energy to healthy choices**. Redirecting your body can redirect and distract your mind. Get busy. Engage in sports, join clubs, take up a hobby, become a volunteer for organizations that help others, exercise, try meditation or yoga or other stress-reduction methods.

·**Be patient and stay focused on your goal**. Managing sexual addiction is a life-long commitment. It's up to you to stay focused on the most important things in your life and to maintain or repair damaged relationships. You can do this. Your entire healthcare team is ready to help you. Choose to let them.

Here are some tips to aid yourself or someone you know that might be struggling to overcome Sex Addiction to avoid relapse and maintain prevention:

1. **Partnering** – you need someone to walk through this process of recovery with you. This person should be an addict as well or at least has recovered from some type of addiction.

2. **Accountability** – seek out support through family, friends, peer support groups, professional counseling, etc. Make sure that several people in your life are aware of your addiction, including your triggers and goals. This will help particularly in social situations when facing temptation.

3. **Predicting** – keep a record to track your behavior patterns, you can call this a "prediction journal" or any other name that fits your overall goals. The main point is for reflection upon progress versus regression.

4. **Distractions** – identify what works for you, everyone has preferred interests, passions, and self-soothing techniques. If you have trouble with creating effective distractions, then seek out advice. Always distract yourself away from any potential sexual exposure that could be triggering.

5. **Exercising** – this stomps out depression and acts as a form of antidepressant that stimulates endorphins "the happy cells" in your brain. These endorphins also get released when you feed into your

addiction, therefore using exercise can replace it.

6. **Securing –** we all have items that we hold onto for consolation purposes. The sensations from attachment, security, and safety can be felt when we have our consoling devices. Whether it is a pet or a childhood keepsake, these items can be very helpful when fighting against an urge to relapse.

7. **Helping –** there is power in knowledge, try reading books about this topic such as "Out of the Shadows: Understanding Sexual Addiction" by Patrick Carnes, learn and teach others, become an expert in how to overcome sex addiction, you will notice a shift of hope with your struggles once you start helping someone else

8. **Praying –** whether you do or do not believe in a god or higher power, there is a sense of relief you will experience after crying or screaming out "help." For those of you who are believers, then you know that prayer can be powerful. Ask others to pray with you when possible.

9. **Seek Out Help –** contact a mental health professional for individual and/or family counseling. Another great resource is support group where you can meet other people experiencing the same struggles with their addiction.

Just remember doing nothing is better than relapsing and giving into your addiction. It is completely normal to be stagnant at times. Take one day at a time and avoid looking too far ahead into the future. Try accepting the things you cannot change and focus on the things you can change

What outcome can I expect if I'm a sex addict?

Although there isn't a cure for sex addiction, if you recognize it and want to end your excessive thoughts, desires, urges and behaviors, it can be effectively managed. It requires your life-long commitment, just as it would for other types of addictions.

If your sexual appetite and activities are causing you distress, consuming your life and causing harm to your personal, professional and/or family life, it's time to have a talk with your healthcare professional. Many people don't seek care because they're ashamed or feel guilty. Your healthcare team makes no judgment about your sexual behavior. They're here to help you. The best outcome will be reached if you're honest and open with everyone — your family, your partner, your medical team and most importantly, yourself. Many treatment options are available to help you..........

ELEVEN

IS LOVE ♡ ADDICTION REAL?

Being in love can bring on a rollercoaster of powerful, sometimes even overwhelming, emotions. The rush of excitement, joy, and other positive feelings love can spark may, for some people, kindle the desire to chase after that experience again and again.

Love addiction creates fixations and compulsions in love interests and can play itself out in unhealthy behaviors toward loved ones. Love addicts can people please, putting the needs of others before their own. It can also result in divorce, affairs, poor job performance, relationship conflict, poor concentration of everyday tasks, enmeshment, clinginess, and emotional distress including anxiety and depression. Emotional highs such as intense passion, and emotional lows, like intense disappointment or heartbreak can eventually strain the relationship, resulting in resentment. Consequently, love addiction may have intense elements of a lack of control present in other addictions, such as sex addiction or a chemical addiction. Love addiction is a controversial and highly debated condition. Some may argue we are all at risk of having some level of love addiction potential. Despite the many opinions on the matter, love addiction can cause emotional problems and even contribute to the breakdown of a relationship. Furthermore, it is a condition that creates much emotional distress, compulsive behaviors and even obsessions where love, romance and sex are concerned. As a result, people battling love addiction can find themselves in unstable relationships, such as toxic or abusive relationships, which can be abusive both mentally and physically. Unfortunately, many may not be able to identify the dangers that come along with such unions.

Love addiction can cause emotional problems and even contribute to the breakdown of a relationship.

Underlying Reasons

Much research is being done to provide information on how love addiction truly works. Genetics, trauma, and upbringing can play a factor in love addition and addiction in general. Love addiction stems from several places like low self-esteem, or other underlying problems. For example, a partner lacking self-esteem may lean on their partner to give them that. Additionally, people may develop love addiction as a way to fill a void left over from childhood trauma, low self-worth, or a lack of self-love. Like other types of addictions, it can stem from abandonment fears. Furthermore, lust for a partner can create obsessiveness as chemicals are released through sexual activity. Sex releases chemicals like oxytocin, and can create an intense attachment for someone who already has low self-esteem or codependency.

An additional reason can include using relationships to fill emotional voids. People may feel love would bring life, excitement, and value. In this case, someone can put too much pressure on their partner to be their everything, have poor emotional boundaries, and develop codependent unions. Feeling like someone has all the traits you lack can cause you to see your partner in an idealized light, or constantly seek approval from their partner. Finally, childhood trauma can be a factor. Circumstances like child abuse, rejection, and emotional neglect can contribute to love addiction.

What are the signs?

Experts do recognize that certain patterns of behavior can become problematic, even addictive. To date, the "Diagnostic and Statistical Manual of Mental Disorders, 5th edition (DSM-5)" recognizes gambling disorder and internet gaming disorder as behavioral addictions.

Yet since love addiction isn't an official diagnosis, you won't find it in the DSM-5. Experts also haven't established any official criteria or symptoms that characterize this behavior pattern.

That said, a few key patterns in your relationship behavior might invite some deeper exploration. If you've noticed any of the signs below, it may be worth connecting with a mental health professional for support.

Intrusive thoughts

It's typical to find your mind preoccupied with a love interest during the "honeymoon phase," when you're first falling for someone, explains Omar Ruiz, licensed therapist and founder of TalkThinkThrive.

But if pervasive thoughts about a particular person, or the idea of love in general, start to negatively affect your job, schoolwork, sleep, or any other areas of your life, that may pose some cause for concern.

Separation anxiety

Missing a partner is very common. But if you feel unbearable distress when they're not around, Ruiz says that may signal what some call love addiction — an unhealthy fixation, in other words.

You may even find yourself avoiding circumstances that would separate you from your love interest, says Gail Saltz, MD, a psychiatrist and clinical associate professor of psychiatry at The NewYork-Presbyterian Hospital.

For example, you might:
>skip work
>ditch school
>cancel plans with friends
>avoid following through on family commitments

Serial monogamy

Do you move from relationship to relationship, not out of fear of being alone, but from an overwhelming or insatiable desire to feel loved? DeMaria says that may point to an unhealthy preoccupation.

Using love as a tool for avoidance

Maybe you find yourself spending a lot of time with the person you love, and you focus on thoughts of them when you can't be together to avoid painful or unwanted thoughts and feelings.

Thinking about a love object as a way of avoiding negative emotions can be a red flag, Ruiz says.

Staying with someone, even when it's unhealthy

Even when a relationship becomes potentially toxic or beyond repair, you may make frantic efforts to maintain it, DeMaria says. But these attempts to keep the relationship alive may prove self-defeating.

Not every relationship will work out, of course, and sometimes moving on is the best option for you and your continued well-being.

Only getting enjoyment out of love or a relationship

Do you mostly only feel positive emotions when in love or with a significant other? That could suggest an unhealthy behavior pattern, Simonian says.

Maybe you find yourself:

·no longer enjoying hobbies or activities that used to excite you

·centering on your partner or relationship as a reason to live

·grappling with feelings of hopelessness when you aren't with your partner

What drives this behavior pattern?

Although experts agree across the board that you can't actually become addicted to relationships, or love in general, many relationship and post-breakup patterns can certainly resemble addiction.

This has a lot to do with your brain chemistry.

For instance, Saltz says you may become determined to get back together with an ex to re-experience those pleasurable feelings associated with love. This shares some similarities with the cravings experienced by people living with substance use disorders.

> "Research from 2016Trusted Source suggested feelings of intense romantic love activate regions of the brain's "reward system" — the same regions engaged with substance use disorders.
>
> Since romantic love activates this system, people in love may experience many of the same behaviors associated with substance use disorders, including cravings and withdrawal.
>
> But it's essential to keep one important distinction in mind: A 2017 studyTrusted Source suggested this effect on the brain lasts much longer in response to substance use than it does in response to love."

Addictive substances, including alcohol, nicotine, and many recreational drugs, trigger the release of a feel-good brain chemical called dopamine, and evidenceTrusted Source suggests love can do the same.

Basically, dopamine tells your brain, "This feels great! Let's do it again!" Saltz says.

Simonian explains the "love addiction" can leave someone unable to focus on anything except being with their partner and the accompanying romantic feelings, which disrupts day-to-day functioning.

"This interruption of functioning is what makes this behavior like an addiction," Simonian says.

According to a 2021 study, certain stages of romantic love can cause an experience that resembles withdrawal.

Saltz notes that a breakup, in particular, may cause some of the same symptoms involved in withdrawalTrusted Source, including:

>anxiety

>trouble sleeping

>changes in appetite

>a low mood and feelings of depression

But again, since love "addiction" doesn't represent an actual addiction, these symptoms can't be compared to the experience of true withdrawal from a substance you physically depend on.

"The abrupt change in routine and loss of receiving affection, paired with decreased levels of dopamine in the brain, might feel like withdrawal," Simonian says. "However, withdrawal from discontinuing drug or alcohol use can cause serious physical symptoms that don't line up with the emotional intensity of a breakup."

These withdrawal-like symptoms are usually rooted in grief, DeMaria says, since the end of a relationship can feel like a devastating loss.

Attachment can also play a part

According to Simonian, a fixation or reliance on romantic relationships can often happen as a symptom of other concerns, like:

·depression

·anxiety

·low self-esteem

·childhood trauma

According to Saltz, this preoccupation often stems from attachment issues. These potentially self-destructive patterns can develop as a result of how you were treated in the past, especially by caregivers.

"Past relationships, particularly ones formed during childhood, tend to set a template for your attachment patterns with others," DeMaria explains. "People often attempt to replicate or resolve issues stemming from their early attachment patterns in their current relationships. This can lead to repeating painful emotional experiences in relationships that feel 'familiar.'"

According to attachment theory, four main types of attachment describe how you view relationships and behave within them.

Anxious-insecure attachment, which seems to stem from inconsistent attention from caregivers, often involves:

·strong cravings for intimacy
·an overdependence on relationships
·frequent relationship insecurity or anxiety
·a fear of abandonment

Some of these tendencies may resemble an "addiction," so to speak, because they lead you to fixate on someone else as a means of avoiding anxiety and other unwanted emotions.

How to cope

Since one of the hallmarks of this fixation is persistent, even all-consuming thoughts of love and relationships, Simonian advises finding other interests that you can focus your energy on.

That could mean any number of possibilities, of course. Ideally, you'll want to opt for activities that mentally engage you and help promote a sense of self-worth.

You can also try engaging in activities that increase those same "happy hormones" as love, including:

>praying
>exercising

>getting a motivational message

>watching a movie that makes you laugh

"It's also helpful to find ways to self-soothe so you aren't relying on others for your sense of emotional well-being," Simonian says. She suggests a few examples of self-soothing coping skills, including:

·meditation

·journaling

·breathing exercise

When to get support

If pursuing or maintaining relationships is disrupting your happiness, health, or ability to complete day-to-day responsibilities, Saltz recommends reaching out to a mental health professional.

How can therapy help?

According to DeMaria, a therapist can offer support with:

·uncovering the underlying cause of your preoccupation with love

·finding new ways to practice self-love and self-care

·addressing unhelpful and unwanted behavior patterns

·building up self-esteem, which can promote a healthier approach to future relationships.

Your therapist might recommend different strategies or techniques, depending on what they determine lies behind these relationship behavior patterns.

That said, Saltz notes they might commonly use therapy approaches like cognitive behavioral therapy (CBT) and dialectical behavioral therapy (DBT).

CBT can help address persistent thought patterns driving compulsive behaviors, while DBT can help you learn new strategies for managing and coping with emotional distress instantly and more effectively regulating emotions in the future.

The bottom line

While you can't actually be "addicted" to love, you can certainly become emotionally dependent on romantic relationships so much that it negatively affects your well-being.

If your preoccupation with pursuing or being in love starts to challenge your ability to work, maintain relationships with friends and family, or take care of yourself physically, a good next step involves connecting with a therapist.

A therapist can offer compassionate guidance with identifying the cause of these thought patterns and behaviors and developing helpful coping strategies.

Constantly Chasing the (Euphoria/Happiness)of New Love? Here's Why It's Not an 'Addiction'

When people say they "have an addiction," they're often talking about an extreme fondness for something. Sure, you might really love snowboarding, listening to podcasts, or watching cat videos. But generally speaking, these aren't actual addictions.

Addiction is a serious condition that affects the brain. True addiction makes it difficult to think about anything else. You're compelled to keep seeking that thing out, even when your need negatively affects you or your loved ones.

This description can make it easy to translate certain relationship behaviors into a "relationship addiction."

These behaviors might include:

>feeling incomplete without a partner

>constantly talking about falling in love

>having more interest in being in love than in sustaining a healthy relationship

>But can you actually be addicted to love? It's complicated.

The idea of relationship addiction is somewhat controversial

Addiction typically refers to alcohol or substance dependency, but experts increasingly support the existence of behavioral addictions. These include addictions to things like gambling and shopping. Relationship addiction, some argue, could fit into this category.
But it's not that simple.
According to Vicki Botnick, a marriage and family therapist in Tarzana, California, "using the term addiction to talk about love and sex is controversial." Love and sex are both a natural part of human life, unlike, say, substance use or gambling.
The lack of diagnostic criteria also complicates things. "Are you an addict when you jump from relationship to relationship? What does 'loving too much' actually mean?" she asks.
In other words, simply moving from relationship to relationship or wanting to have multiple relationships at the same time doesn't mean you're "addicted." Neither does falling in love quickly, wanting to find a new partner immediately after a breakup, or enjoying how it feels to have a relationship.
Still, Botnick acknowledges that, "as with any condition, it's concerning when someone's thoughts and behavior cause significant, ongoing distress."

Still, there's some evidence that relationships can be addictive

A few recent studies have explored how characteristics of addiction can show up in the development of romantic relationships.
A 2016 study Trusted Source describes romantic love as a natural addiction. People in love often experience euphoria, cravings, dependency, withdrawal, and other behaviors associated with addiction. This happens, researchers explain, because the dopamine reward system in your brain is activated by romantic love, just as it's activated by substances and addictive behaviors. However, the

authors make the distinction that romantic love isn't characterized as a behavioral or chemical addiction.

A 2018 review and case study echoed the link between love and dopamine. However, the authors noted that the cravings and longing tend to mellow over time into a more stable, lasting love. That is, when the love is mutual. One-sided or unrequited love might feel more addictive.

The addictive qualities of love can also come into play during a breakup. A 2010 study examined brain activity in 15 people who had recently experienced relationship rejection. According to the study, similar areas of the brain activated by cocaine cravings were also activated after rejection.

Where it might come from

As with other types of addiction, addiction-like behaviors around relationships result from a complex interaction of factors. These include brain chemistry, genetics, upbringing, and the relationships you see around you.

Others argue that love is simply an evolutionary survival response. Botnick also points to low self-esteem as a key contributor. "When we don't know how to get positive feedback from inside ourselves, we need it from outside sources. Falling in love, or just getting interest from potential partners, can become a method we rely on." She also adds that attachment issues can fuel this pattern.

Signs to look for

Although relationship addiction isn't recognized as an official diagnosis, mental health experts and existing research generally agree on a few key signs that suggest cause for concern.

You need to keep falling in love

Experts link the euphoric high (activated by the release of dopamine and other "happy" hormones) that's so common in the early stages of love to addictive relationship behaviors. So it follows that someone experiencing this pattern would crave that feeling again and again.

"You might find yourself in a revolving door of relationships, with no down time in between," explains Melissa Stringer, a marriage and family therapist in Sunnyvale, Texas"

You want the excitement of early love, but you don't want to stick around for a relationship. This can hurt both you and your romantic partners over time, especially when you don't communicate (or realize) your relationship goals.

You continue "craving" someone who doesn't feel the same way

"With all addictions or comfort-seeking behaviors, an obsessive type of focus can begin to take over," Stringer says.

Maybe you struggle to let go of a relationship after it ends. Or you might fixate on the person you love, even if they no longer return your feelings. Even after they ask for space, you might feel compelled to keep seeing them, trying to convince them to give the relationship another chance.

This overwhelming need for your partner can also happen within a relationship when you crave their company so much you neglect work, school, and other important parts of your life in order to spend time together.

You idealize the idea of love

According to Botnick, unrealistic cultural ideas about love can play a part.

"From fairy tales to Lifetime movies to Facebook feeds, we're bombarded with images of 'perfect' partners and love that 'completes' us," she says.

With these ideals in mind, you might feel like you have to keep searching for that soulmate, that perfect love, without considering the very real work that goes into making a relationship strong and successful.

You don't care who you date, as long as you're in a relationship

Many people who struggle with compulsive relationship behaviors need others to build up their self-worth. If you find it hard to love yourself or make yourself happy, you might look for someone to fulfill that need.

This consuming need for a relationship can make it easier to end up with someone who isn't the best match. It could even have a harmful impact if you stay in an abusive or toxic relationship to avoid being single.

Your relationships follow a similar pattern

Relationship addiction can involve a lot of breaking up and getting back together.

"The beginning of a relationship releases endorphins and dopamine, which feel wonderful, while breakups can spike a deep depression. People with certain personality types may feel attracted to this roller coaster and have a hard time feeling alive without it," Botnick explains.

Stringer expands on this, suggesting that the enthusiasm of believing you've found "the one" and depression when the short-lived relationship ends can form a cycle. This cycle can lead to impulsive decisions and affect your ability to function as you usually would.

Tips for overcoming it

If you're working to address compulsive love or relationship behaviors, awareness of how these behaviors affect you is an essential first step.

But, Stringer emphasizes, awareness usually isn't enough. "Learning new skills and tools for coping are both necessary parts of behavior change," she explains.

These tips can help you begin creating that change.

Try a reality check

If you tend to idealize love, try looking at your relationships through a more realistic lens.

Love can be great, it's true. A committed partner can provide emotional support, a sense of connection and belonging, and help meet other needs. But a partner can't meet all of your needs.

Thriving relationships are interdependent. That means you have an established self-identity and don't lose it in the relationship. You can work to get your own needs met but also know when to look to your partner for help and support.

> *"Remember that healthy relationships take work. In the beginning, things usually seem easy: You have great chemistry, share interests, and never argue. But over time, as you get more comfortable, your differences might begin to stand out."*

This doesn't mean the relationship has failed. It just means you have to work together to learn more about each other and find a middle ground.

Take a break from relationships

When problematic patterns arise in your relationships, it's helpful to step back and consider why the same things keep happening.

Dissatisfaction often means you aren't getting what you need. But maybe you aren't exactly sure what you need or want. Or perhaps you're searching for something you're unlikely to find (like romanticized love that mostly only exists in the media).

Remember, forming and quickly ending relationships doesn't just affect you. It can also affect the partners you leave behind.

If you don't want to continue a relationship, you should never feel compelled or obligated to do so. However, you owe it to potential partners (and yourself) to be as honest and clear about your intentions as possible, if you want to avoid causing harm.

Spending time with friends and family can help you prioritize other strong relationships. The bonds you have with other loved ones can fulfill other important social connection needs besides romance.

Practice loving yourself

Self-love is tied to self-esteem, and a lack of either can contribute to relationship dependency and addiction-like behaviors.

Working to build up self-esteem on your own isn't always easy, but Botnick suggests:

·**Asking yourself if you have realistic standards for yourself.** If not, try to identify more moderate, achievable goals. Unrealistic goals can lead to self-criticism and self-blame when you fail to achieve them.

·**Identifying negative self-talk.** If you find yourself thinking something like, "I'll never have the love I want," try replacing it with something more realistic such as, "Exploring what I want from a relationship can help me find what I'm looking for."

Positive self-talk can also help you feel better about yourself and lead to stronger relationships.

When to get help

Addictive behaviors around love, sex, and relationships can be hard to overcome on your own.

According to Stringer, a number of factors can affect your success in moving past these behaviors without professional help. "When unresolved trauma drives these behaviors," she says, "chances are lower you'll simply be able to stop them."

If you're having difficulty, a therapist can help. Therapy is always recommended whenever relationship behaviors cause you (or anyone) distress.

It's best to talk to someone sooner rather than later if you:

> depend entirely on your partner
> believe your life lacks meaning without a relationship
> feel unable to leave a toxic relationship
> can't stop calling or texting a love interest or past partner who's asked you not to contact them
> have thoughts of hurting yourself or someone else
> experience significant, lasting mood changes, like depression or irritability

A therapist can work with you to identify and address thought patterns or underlying issues contributing to these feelings and behaviors.

Therapy can also help you develop stronger relationships. If your craving for the euphoric "high" of new love is keeping you from the long-term relationship you actually desire, a therapist can help you come up with a productive plan for creating the kind of love you're seeking.

The bottom line

Some experts suggestTrusted Source we're all addicted to love. After all, we need to connect with others to continue our existence, so we want — even crave — these bonds throughout our lives.

The need for love or a relationship doesn't affect everyone negatively. It's completely normal and healthy to want a relationship, and if your search for love doesn't harm you or anyone else, you likely don't need to worry.

But if you feel dependent on relationships, or if your relationship patterns or behaviors concern you in other ways, a therapist can offer support without judgment.

Love Bombing: Signs of Over-the-Top Love

When you first meet someone, being swept off your feet can feel fun and exciting. Having someone shower you with affection and admiration is especially exhilarating when you're in the beginning stages of a new relationship.

Love bombing, however, is another story. It happens when someone overwhelms you with loving words, actions, and behavior as a manipulation technique.

"It's often used to win over your trust and affection so that they can meet a goal of theirs," explains Shirin Peykar, MA, a licensed marriage and family therapist.

Here's a look at some of the classic love bombing signs. If you recognize some of these, it doesn't necessarily mean your partner is toxic, but listen to your intuition if the person trying to woo you seems too good to be true

They lavish you with gifts

Love bombing often involves over-the-top gestures, such as sending you inappropriate gifts to your job (dozens of bouquets instead of one, for example) or buying expensive plane tickets for a vacation, and not taking "no" for an answer.

All of this can seem harmless enough, but the point is to manipulate you into thinking you owe them something.

"Most often, love bombing is done by a narcissist with the intent of drawing in and gaining control over the person who is being love bombed," says licensed professional counselor Tabitha Westbrook, LMFT.

They can't stop complimenting you

We all crave admiration, but constant praise can make your head spin. If someone's expressing their undying love after just a short amount of time, it's a potential red flag that their feelings aren't genuine.

Some common, over-the-top phrases they might use include:
- "I love everything about you."
- "I've never met anyone as perfect as you."
- "You're the only person I want to spend time with."

On their own, these phrases aren't necessarily harmful, but it's important to consider them in the larger context of someone's overall behavior.

They bombard you with phone calls and texts

They call, text, and message you over social media 24/7. While being in constant communication is normal when you're first dating, it's a red flag if the communication feels one-sided and becomes increasingly overwhelming.

Take note if they begin texting you early in the morning and every hour on the hour

They want your undivided attention

When your focus isn't on the other person, they might become angry. This can look like pouting when you're on the phone with friends or refusing to leave after you say you have to be at work early the next day.

> *"True love does not want all your time and energy focused on them alone," Westbrook emphasizes. "They respect other commitments, ideas, and boundaries."*

They try to convince you that you're soulmates

Telling you they dreamed that God told them you two should marry is a manipulation tactic. If what they say sounds right out of a film, take heed, Westbrook notes. "Hollywood is great for entertainment, but true love and relationships don't look like the movies."
Some other things they might say:
   •"We were born to be together."
   •"It's fate that we met."
   •"You understand me more than anyone."
   •"We're soulmates."

They want commitment and they want it now

A love bomber might pressure you into rushing things and making big plans for the future. They'll mention things like marriage or moving in together when you've only known each other a short while.
The thing to keep in mind, according to Westbrook, is that real relationships take time to develop. "It's very unlikely the person really can love you more than anything in the world in 2 weeks. Or two days. Or 2 hours. Or even 2 months," she explains.

They get upset when you place boundaries

When you try to tell them to slow down, they'll continue to try to manipulate you to get what they want. Someone who legitimately cares, on the other hand, will respect your wishes and back off.
"Love bombers also get upset about any boundaries with regard to access to you or you accepting their displays of 'love,' says Westbrook. "It's like a tsunami of affection and they expect you to accept it all."

They're overly needy

No matter how much time and access you give them, it never seems to be enough. But ask yourself: Are you bailing on friends because they can't stand to Heading 2be alone? Or do you feel obligated to answer every text because they gifted you that expensive iPhone? LOL
Someone toxic will make you feel indebted to them so that they can rely on you day and night.

You're overwhelmed by their intensity

They never turn down the charm and seem to be running on all cylinders when you're with them. You never know what to expect from one moment to the next and feel pressured into seeing them round the clock.
Legitimate love has its ups and downs, but it's respectful and not overbearing, says Westbrook. "It is patient, kind, and gentle."

You feel unbalanced

Being love bombed can feel intoxicating at first, but you might also feel a bit uneasy, waiting for the other shoe to drop.
Pay attention to these anxious feelings, says Westbrook. It's important to be attuned to your intuition, so you can be informed instead of being carried away by love bombing tactics.

The bottom line

If you're in the early stages of a relationship and everything feels like it's happening too soon, check in with your gut. Remember: Falling in love should be savored, not rushed.
If you're worried your partner has crossed into manipulative territory, try reaching out to a trusted friend, family member, or mental health therapist who can help you assess their behavior.

You can also check out the below resources for additional guidance on next steps:

•**Love is Respect** is a national dating abuse helpline that offers support and provides information on unhealthy relationships and behaviors.

•**One Love** is a foundation helping put a stop to relationship abuse

What's (Unconditional) Love Got to Do with It?

Unconditional love, simply put, is love without strings attached. It's love you offer freely.

You don't base it on what someone does for you in return. You simply love them and want nothing more than their happiness.

This type of love, sometimes called compassionate or agape love, might sound somewhat familiar. Maybe it brings to mind the love your parents have for you or the love you have for your own child.

While people often associate unconditional love with familial love, many look for this love in romantic relationships, too.

Wanting someone to love you for yourself — no matter what — is an understandable desire. Yet this type of love might still seem like the stuff of fairy tales and movies, not something most people encounter in real life.

Is this love as elusive as it sounds? Can it even happen in romantic relationships?

Read on for a deeper understanding of what unconditional love is (and isn't) and some strategies for cultivating it.

What it is

Unconditional love is a selfless act. You're not in it for yourself.

Though it may overlap with other types of love in some ways, other elements set it apart.

You can recognize it by these key characteristics.

It can benefit emotional health

A small 2009 study explored the brain regions activated by feelings of unconditional love. The results of the study suggest that unconditional love activates some of the same areas of the brain's reward system that romantic love does.

In other words, the simple act of loving someone unconditionally may produce positive feelings.

Receiving unconditional love can also make a difference in emotional well-being. According to research from 2010, children who receive higher levels of affection from their parents or caregivers tend to have greater resilience in adulthood. They also tend to experience fewer mental health symptoms.

Results from a 2013 study support the idea that loving children unconditionally improves their lifelong health and wellness. This suggests parental unconditional love could offer some protection against the harmful, often lingering effects of childhood trauma or abuse.

It feels secure

Unconditional love can provide a sense of security in both childhood and adulthood.

Feeling confident in someone's love and knowing it won't go away can help create secure attachments and foster autonomy, independence, and self-worth.

If you know your parents or caregivers will continue to love you even after you make mistakes or do things they don't approve of — from failing a class to having a drink at a party when you're underage — you'll feel more comfortable making your own choices and learning from them as you go.

In the context of friendship, unconditional love might weather tests like conflict, falling out of touch, or differing life goals.

When it comes to romantic relationships, unconditional love could mean that love doesn't go away, despite challenges like life-altering health conditions or changes in appearance or personality.

It's altruistic

Altruism refers to helpful actions taken to support and benefit others, often at your own expense.

In terms of unconditional love, altruism means you don't consider any potential benefits of loving someone. You offer your love for their support and benefit.

Love, many say, is its own reward, but you typically don't get anything out of altruistic acts. This is one point of contention in discussions of unconditional love in romantic situations.

Because healthy relationships, by definition, are mutually beneficial, this would seem to suggest that romantic love — at least within the boundaries of a relationship — can't be truly unconditional.

It involves acceptance and forgiveness

People aren't perfect, and nearly everyone makes a few choices they regret. Unconditional love, however, requires unconditional acceptance.

So, you forgive mistakes and continue to offer love and acceptance, even — and this is important — if their choices distress you or cause harm.

You can't love someone unconditionally unless your love remains unchanged despite their actions. You can, however, love someone unconditionally without having a relationship with them.

Acceptance sometimes involves recognizing when it's unlikely someone will change and taking steps to protect your own well-being.

What it isn't

Confusion and misconceptions about the true nature of unconditional love can seem to suggest this type of love reflects unhealthy or toxic relationship dynamics.

> *"There's an important distinction between offering love and forgiveness and continuing to accept harmful actions. It's also important to understand you can love someone unconditionally without staying with them unconditionally."*

To clear things up a bit more, here's what unconditional love does not mean.

Ignoring relationship issues

Conflict is normal (and healthy) in relationships. Unconditional love doesn't mean you avoid this conflict or look away from problematic behavior.

Say your partner spends your joint savings on an expensive exercise bike — a choice you completely disagree with — when you'd agreed to save up for a house. You might not stop loving them, but neither do you ignore the breach of trust.

Depending on the circumstances, you might agree to work together on rebuilding trust (and your savings), but you might also see no future in the relationship. You can walk away still holding forgiveness and love in your heart.

Neglecting your own needs

It's true that unconditional love can involve some sacrifice, but these sacrifices shouldn't require you to give up everything you need and want for yourself.

Attempting to meet all your partner's needs can seem like one way of expressing unconditional love, but this can actually create an unhealthy dynamic in your relationship. No one person can provide another person with everything they need.

You should feel comfortable setting boundaries around things you don't want to do. What's more, they should respect your limits and consider any requests you make.

When they can't provide the support you need, they might offer a potential compromise or help you think of some other solution.

Even when your love doesn't depend on their ability to meet your needs, you still have those needs — everyone does.

Unconditional love can't fuel a healthy relationship on its own. It's essential to take care of your own needs, too, or you won't be in any position to support someone else.

Tolerating abuse

A sense of safety is a basic human need.

Perhaps your partner says unkind things after drinking. You might tell yourself, "They wouldn't shout at me if they weren't drunk." You might accept that this is who they are and make the choice to forgive their words and continue loving them.

But unconditional love doesn't mean staying in an unhealthy situation when you're better off letting go.

You want them to be happy, but what if quitting drinking and dealing with the issues that trigger the urge to drink would improve their health and help them find greater happiness?

Again, you can offer forgiveness and love even after safely leaving the relationship.

Blanket tolerance for harmful behavior can prevent them from making needed changes. Though remember that this absolutely doesn't mean you're to blame. The responsibility for their actions rests entirely in their hands.

Is it even possible?

If you're starting to think unconditional love sounds a lot more complicated than you'd imagined, you've pretty much hit the mark.

As one philosophy professor pointed out, even the love between a parent and a child falls short of unconditional. A parent might love their child no matter what they do, but this love still has a condition: They love their child because their child is theirs.

In a similar vein, consider the love you have for your partner or anyone else. What triggered it originally? Perhaps you felt attracted to certain specific characteristics: sense of humor, a kind heart, intelligence.

If they no longer had those characteristics, would your love continue, unaltered? From a philosophical perspective, if conditions never change, you might never know whether your love truly is unconditional.

In reality, love grows and shifts over time. It can also fade, through no fault of anyone involved. Love changes, in part, because people change. You, or your partner, may not be the same person years down the line.

> "*Instead of seeking out an idealized, potentially unattainable type of love, try for a better, more realistic, goal: mature love founded on compassion and respect.*"

Fostering it in your relationship

While a parent may love their child from the moment of birth, romantic love can take a little more time and effort.

These strategies can help you nurture and sustain deep, lasting love.

Offer respect, even when you disagree

You and your partner are two different people, so it makes sense you'll have a difference of opinion at some point.

Many people think of conflict as something negative, but it isn't always bad. It can even improve the health of your relationship when handled in a productive way.

When navigating conflict, it's important to accept any differences with respect. You want to send a message that says, "I disagree with you, but I still respect your opinion."

Once you both express your opinions, you can begin working toward resolution. This might involve collaboration or compromise. Without respect, though, it'll be tough.

Practice open communication

Good communication should be clear, honest, and timely. All the honest, open sharing in the world may not make much difference if it comes too late.

By communicating with your partner, you show your respect and commitment to working through challenges and finding ways to meet conflicting goals.

For better communication:

·Bring up issues as they arise instead of letting your irritation simmer and gather heat.

·Share your thoughts honestly, but also listen empathically to what your partner has to say.

·Make sure to clarify when you don't understand something to better prevent conflict in the future.

If you're not used to communicating in this way (plenty of us aren't), be patient. Things will get easier with practice.

Support each other

Most relationships that thrive involve plenty of mutual support.

When your partner struggles, you listen with empathy or offer a helping hand, and they do the same for you. You stay mindful of their needs as well as your own, and they know you have their back when they're up against something they can't handle alone.

A time may come when you find yourself sacrificing something for their benefit, but sacrifice and support should go both ways. A healthy relationship involves not just take, but also some give — so they'll likely make sacrifices for your benefit, too.

The bottom line

Unconditional love might sound like a dream come true. But while love is one thing, a relationship is quite another.

A healthy relationship does have conditions, of a sort: your boundaries. If your partner doesn't respect your boundaries, the relationship isn't healthy, no matter how deeply you love them.

Moving on from it, then, could be an act of unconditional self-love.

LOVE

VERSUS

LOVE-ADDICTION

COMPARING 2 TYPES OF RELATIONSHIPS

LOVE	LOVE ADDICTION
Love feels: calming, relaxing, stabilizing, supportive	Love Addiction feels: intense, thrilling, electrifying, like an emotional roller coaster, infatuation at first sight
Love is: slow and steady, cultivated over time, grounded in trust, respectful of boundaries, independence, and healthy interdependence	Love Addiction is: immersive, impulsive, fast moving, based on fantasy and projection, void of emotional intimacy, unsustainable
Love encourages: being your best self, having time and space alone, generating a sense of wholeness from within, clear, compassionate, and direct communication	Love Addiction involves: ride or die behavior, codependence, control, projection, suspicion, paranoia, lying, spying, playing out unresolved childhood wounds, fear of spending time alone, boundary issues, unclear communication, self-abandonment, blame, deflection, avoiding responsibility

love vs love

TWELVE

IS ADDICTION TO FOOD A DISORDER?

Food addiction is an addiction to junk food and comparable to drug addiction.

It's a relatively new — and controversial — term, and high quality statistics on its prevalence are lacking.

Food addiction is similar to several other disorders, including binge eating disorder, bulimia, compulsive overeating, and other feeding and eating disorders.

"SUMMARY
Food addiction is a highly controversial concept, though most studies suggest it exists. It works similarly to drug addiction"

The idea that a person can be addicted to food has recently gained increasing support. That comes from brain imaging and other studies of the effects of compulsive overeating on pleasure centers in the brain.

Experiments in animals and humans show that, for some people, the same reward and pleasure centers of the brain that are triggered by addictive drugs like cocaine and heroin are also activated by food, especially highly palatable foods. Highly palatable foods are foods rich in:

·Sugar

·Fat

·salt

Like addictive drugs, highly palatable foods trigger feel-good brain chemicals such as dopamine. Once people experience pleasure associated with increased dopamine transmission in the brain's reward pathway from eating certain foods, they quickly feel the need to eat again.

The reward signals from highly palatable foods may override other signals of fullness and satisfaction. As a result, people keep eating, even when they're not hungry. Compulsive overeating is a type of behavioral addiction meaning that someone can become preoccupied with a behavior (such as eating, or gambling, or shopping) that triggers intense pleasure. People with food addictions lose control over their eating behavior and find themselves spending excessive amounts of time involved with food and overeating, or anticipating the emotional effects of compulsive overeating.

People who show signs of food addiction may also develop a kind of tolerance to food. They eat more and more, only to find that food satisfies them less and less.

Scientists believe that food addiction may play an important role in obesity. But normal-weight people may also struggle with food addiction. Their bodies may simply be genetically programmed to better handle the extra calories they take in. Or they may increase their physical activity to compensate for overeating.

People who are addicted to food will continue to eat despite negative consequences, such as weight gain or damaged relationships. And like people who are addicted to drugs or gambling, people who are addicted to food will have trouble stopping their behavior, even if they want to or have tried many times to cut back.

While food addiction is not listed in the Diagnostic and Statistical Manual of Mental Disorders (DSM-5), it typically involves binge eating behaviors, cravings, and a lack of control around food. While someone who gets a craving or overeats occasionally probably won't fit the criteria for the disorder, there are at least 8 common symptoms.

Here are some common signs and symptoms of food addiction.

1. Getting cravings despite feeling full

It's not uncommon to get cravings, even after eating a fulfilling, nutritious meal.
For example, after eating a dinner with steak, potatoes, and veggies, some people may crave ice cream for dessert.
Cravings and hunger aren't the same thing.
A craving occurs when you experience an urge to eat something, despite having already eaten or being full.
This is pretty common and doesn't necessarily mean that someone has food addiction. Most people get cravings.
However, if cravings happen often and satisfying or ignoring them becomes hard, they may be an indicator of something else.
These cravings are not about a need for energy or nutrients — it's the brain calling for something that releases dopamine, a chemical in the brain that plays a role in how humans feel pleasure.

> "SUMMARY
> Cravings are very common. While a craving alone doesn't indicate food addiction, if you often get cravings and ignoring or satisfying them is difficult, it may indicate a problem."

2. Eating much more than intended

For some people, there is no such thing as a bite of chocolate or single piece of cake. One bite turns into 20, and one slice of cake turns into half a cake.

This all-or-nothing approach is common with addiction of any kind. There is no such thing as moderation — it simply does not work (4Trusted Source).

Telling someone with food addiction to eat junk food in moderation is almost like telling someone with alcoholism to drink beer in moderation. It's just not possible.

> **"SUMMARY**
> *When giving in to a craving, someone with food addiction might eat much more than intended."*

3. Eating until feeling excessively stuffed

When giving in to a craving, someone with food addiction may not stop eating until the urge is satisfied. They might then realize that they have eaten so much that their stomach feels completely stuffed.

> **"SUMMARY**
> *Eating until feeling excessively stuffed — either frequently or all the time — may be classified as binge eating."*

4. Feeling guilty afterward but doing it again soon

Trying to exert control over the consumption of unhealthy foods and then giving in to a craving can lead to feelings of guilt.

A person may feel that they are doing something wrong or even cheating themselves.

Despite these unpleasant feelings, a person with food addiction will repeat the pattern.

"SUMMARY

Feelings of guilt after a period of binge eating are common."

5. Making up excuses

The brain can be a strange thing, especially in regards to addiction. Deciding to stay away from trigger foods can cause someone to create rules for themselves. Yet, these rules may be hard to follow.
When faced with a craving, someone with food addiction might find ways to reason around the rules and give in to the craving.
This line of thinking may resemble that of a person who is in the process of trying to quit smoking. That person might think that if they don't buy a pack of cigarettes themselves, they're not a smoker. Nonetheless, they might smoke cigarettes from a friend's pack.

"SUMMARY
Setting rules around eating patterns and then making excuses for why it's okay to disregard them can be common with food addiction."

6. Repeated failures at setting rules

When people are struggling with self-control, they often try to set rules for themselves.
Examples include only sleeping in on the weekends, always doing homework right after school, never drinking coffee after a certain time in the afternoon. For most people, these rules almost always fail, and rules around eating are no exception.
Examples include having one cheat meal or cheat day per week and only eating junk food at parties, birthdays, or holidays.

> **"SUMMARY**
> *Many people have at least some history of failing to set rules regarding their food consumption."*

7. Hiding eating from others

People with a history of rule setting and repeated failures often start hiding their consumption of junk food from others.
They may prefer to eat alone, when no one else is home, alone in the car, or late at night after everyone else has gone to bed.

> **"SUMMARY**
> *Hiding food intake is fairly common among people who feel unable to control their consumption."*

8. Unable to quit despite physical problems

Which foods you choose to eat can significantly affect your health.
In the short term, junk food can lead to weight gain, acne, bad breath, fatigue, poor dental health, and other common problems.
A lifetime of junk food consumption can lead to obesity, type 2 diabetes, heart disease, Alzheimer's, dementia, and even some types of cancer.
Someone who experiences any of these problems related to their intake of unhealthy foods but is unable to change their habits likely needs help.
A treatment plan that's designed by qualified professionals is typically recommended for overcoming eating disorders.

> **"SUMMARY**
> *Even when unhealthy eating patterns cause physical issues, it can be hard to stop."*

The bottom line

The DSM-5 is a guide used by health professionals to diagnose mental disorders.

The criteria for substance dependence includes many of the symptoms above. They fit in with medical definitions of addiction. However, the DSM-5 has not established criteria for food addiction. If you have repeatedly tried to quit eating or cut back on your consumption of junk food but can't, it could be an indicator of food addiction.

Fortunately, certain strategies can help you overcome it.

Effects on the brain

Food addiction involves the same areas of the brain as drug addiction. Also, the same neurotransmitters are involved, and many of the symptoms are identical.

Processed junk foods have a powerful effect on the reward centers of the brain. These effects are caused by brain neurotransmitters like dopamine.

The most problematic foods include typical junk foods like candy, sugary soda, and high fat fried foods.

Food addiction is not caused by a lack of willpower but believed to be caused by a dopamine signal that affects the biochemistry of the brain.

> "SUMMARY
> *Food addiction is thought to involve the same neurotransmitters and areas of the brain as drug addiction.*"

It's a serious problem

Though the term addiction is often thrown around lightly, having a true addiction is a serious condition that typically requires treatment to overcome.

The symptoms and thought processes associated with food addiction are similar to those of drug abuse. It's just a different substance, and the social consequences may be less severe.

Food addiction can cause physical harm and lead to chronic health conditions like obesity and type 2 diabetes.

In addition, it may negatively impact a person's self-esteem and self-image, making them unhappy with their body.

As with other addictions, food addiction may take an emotional toll and increase a person's risk of premature death.

> "SUMMARY
> *Food addiction increases the risk of obesity and type 2 diabetes. Excessive weight may also affect a person's self-esteem.*"

How to know whether avoiding junk food is worth the sacrifice

Completely avoiding junk foods may seem impossible. They're everywhere and a major part of modern culture.

However, in some cases, entirely abstaining from certain trigger foods can become necessary.

Once the firm decision to never eat these foods again is made, avoiding them may become easier, as the need to justify eating — or not eating — them is eliminated. Cravings may also disappear or decrease significantly.

Consider writing a list of pros and cons to think through the decision.

Pros. These may include losing weight, living longer, having more energy, and feeling better every day.

Cons. These may include not being able to eat ice cream with family, no cookies during the holiday season, and having to explain food choices.

Write everything down — no matter how peculiar or vain it may seem. Then compare the two lists and ask if it's worth it.

If the answer is a resounding "yes," be assured that it's the right decision.

Also, keep in mind that many of the social dilemmas that may show up in the con list can often easily be solved.

> "*SUMMARY*
> *To overcome food addiction, a person should be sure that eliminating certain foods is the right thing to do. If there's uncertainty, writing down the pros and cons may help make the decision.*"

First steps in overcoming food addiction

A few things can help prepare for giving up junk foods and make the transition easier:

Trigger foods. Write down a list of the foods that cause cravings and/or binges. These are the trigger foods to avoid completely.

Fast food places. Make a list of fast food places that serve healthy foods and note their healthy options. This may prevent a relapse when hungry and not in the mood to cook.

What to eat. Think about what foods to eat — preferably healthy foods that are liked and already eaten regularly.

Pros and cons. Consider making several copies of the pro-and-con list. Keep a copy in the kitchen, glove compartment, and purse or wallet.

Additionally, don't go on a diet. Put weight loss on hold for at least 1–3 months.

Overcoming food addiction is difficult enough. Adding hunger and restrictions to the mix is likely to make things harder.

After taking these preparatory steps, set a date in the near future — like the coming weekend — from which point onward the addictive trigger foods won't be touched again.

"SUMMARY
To overcome food addiction, it's important to plan. Make a list of trigger foods and know what is going to be eaten instead."

Consider seeking help

Most people with addiction attempt to quit several times before they succeed in the long run.

While it's possible to overcome addiction without help — even if it takes several tries — it can often be beneficial to seek help.

Many health professionals and support groups can aid in overcoming your addiction.

Finding a psychologist or psychiatrist who has experience in dealing with food addiction can provide one-on-one support, but there are several free group options available as well.

These include 12-step programs like Overeaters Anonymous (OA), GreySheeters Anonymous (GSA), Food Addicts Anonymous (FAA), and Food Addicts in Recovery Anonymous (FA).

These groups meet regularly — some even via video chat — and can offer the support needed to overcome addiction.

"SUMMARY
Consider seeking help for food addiction. Try support groups like Overeaters Anonymous or book an appointment with a psychologist or psychiatrist who specializes in food addiction."

The bottom line

Food addiction is a problem that rarely resolves on its own. Unless a conscious decision to deal with it is made, chances are it will worsen over time.

The first steps to overcoming the addiction include listing the pros and cons of quitting trigger foods, finding healthy food alternatives, and setting a fixed date to start the journey toward health.

Consider seeking help from a health professional or free support group. Always remember that you're not alone.

The 18 Most Addictive Foods (and the 17 Least Addictive)

Up to 20% of people may have a food addiction or exhibit addictive-like eating behavior. This number is even higher among people with obesity.

Food addiction involves being addicted to food in the same way as someone with a substance use disorder demonstrates addiction to a particular substance.

People who have food addiction report that they are unable to control their consumption of certain foods.

However, people don't just become addicted to any food. Some foods are much more likely to cause symptoms of addiction than others.

Foods that can cause addictive-like eating

Researchers at the University of Michigan studied addictive-like eating in 518 people.

They used the Yale Food Addiction Scale (YFAS) as a reference. It's the most commonly used tool to assess food addiction.

All participants received a list of 35 foods, both processed and unprocessed.

They rated how likely they were to experience problems with each of the 35 foods, on a scale of 1 (not at all addictive) to 7 (extremely addictive).

In this study, 7–10% of participants were diagnosed with full-blown food addiction.

In addition, 92% of participants exhibited addictive-like eating behavior toward some foods. They repeatedly had the desire to quit eating them but were unable to do so.

The results below detail which foods were the most and least addictive.

> **"**SUMMARY
> *In a 2015 study, 92% of participants exhibited addictive-like eating behavior toward certain foods. 7–10% of them met the researchers' criteria for full-blown food addiction.***"***

The 18 most addictive foods

Not surprisingly, most of the foods rated as addictive were processed foods. These foods were usually high in sugar or fat — or both.
The number following each food is the average score given in the study mentioned above, on a scale of 1 (not at all addictive) to 7 (extremely addictive).

pizza (4.01)

chocolate (3.73)

chips (3.73)

cookies (3.71)

ice cream (3.68)

french fries (3.60)

cheeseburgers (3.51)

soda (not diet) (3.29)

cake (3.26)

cheese (3.22)

bacon (3.03)

fried chicken (2.97)

rolls (plain) (2.73)

popcorn (buttered) (2.64)

breakfast cereal (2.59)

gummy candy (2.57)

steak (2.54)
  muffins (2.50)

"SUMMARY
The 18 most addictive foods were most often processed foods with high amounts of fat and added sugar."

The 17 least addictive foods

The least addictive foods were mostly whole, unprocessed foods.

cucumbers (1.53)

carrots (1.60)

beans (no sauce) (1.63)

apples (1.66)

brown rice (1.74)

broccoli (1.74)

bananas (1.77)

salmon (1.84)

corn (no butter or salt) (1.87)

strawberries (1.88)

granola bar (1.93)

water (1.94)

crackers (plain) (2.07)

pretzels (2.13)

chicken breast (2.16)

eggs (2.18)

nuts (2.47)

"SUMMARY
The least addictive foods were almost all whole, unprocessed foods."

What makes junk food addictive?

Addictive-like eating behavior involves a lot more than just a lack of willpower, as there are biochemical reasons why some people lose control over their consumption.

This behavior has repeatedly been linked to processed foods, especially those high in added sugar and/or fat. Processed foods are usually engineered to be hyper-palatable so that they taste really good.

They also contain high amounts of calories and cause significant blood sugar imbalances. These are known factors that can cause food cravings.

However, the biggest contributor to addictive-like eating behavior is the human brain.

Your brain has a reward center that secretes dopamine and other feel-good chemicals when you eat.

This reward center explains why many people enjoy eating. It ensures that enough food is eaten to get all the energy and nutrients that the body needs.

Eating processed junk food releases massive amounts of feel-good chemicals, compared with unprocessed foods. This yields a much more powerful reward in the brain.

The brain then seeks more reward by causing cravings for these hyper-rewarding foods. This can lead to a vicious cycle called addictive-like eating behavior or food addiction.

> "SUMMARY
> *Processed foods can cause blood sugar imbalances and cravings. Eating junk food also makes the brain release feel-good chemicals, which can lead to even more cravings.*"

The bottom line

Food addiction and addictive-like eating behavior can create serious problems, and certain foods are more likely to trigger them.

Eating a diet that mostly comprises whole, single-ingredient foods can help reduce the likelihood of developing a food addiction.

They release an appropriate amount of feel-good chemicals, while not triggering the urge to overeat.

Note that many who have food addiction will need help to overcome it. Working with a therapist can address any underlying psychological issues contributing to food addiction, while a nutritionist can design a diet that's free of trigger foods without depriving the body of nutrition.

How Food Addiction Works (and What to Do About It)

People tend to get cravings when the brain starts calling for certain foods — often processed foods that aren't considered healthy or nutritious.

Even though the conscious mind knows they're unhealthy, some other part of the brain seems to disagree.

Some people don't experience this and can easily control the types of foods they eat, while others can't.

This isn't due to a lack of willpower — it's a much more complex situation.

The fact is junk food stimulates the reward system in the brain in the same way as addictive drugs, such as cocaine.

For susceptible people, eating junk food can lead to full-blown addiction, which shares the same biological basis as drug addiction.

How does food addiction work?

There is a system in the brain called the reward system.

This system was designed to reward the brain when a person is doing things that encourage survival. This includes primal behaviors like eating.

The brain knows that when a person eats, they're doing something right, and it releases feel-good chemicals in the reward system.

These chemicals include the neurotransmitter dopamine, which the brain interprets as pleasure. The brain is hardwired to seek out behaviors that release dopamine in the reward system.

The problem with modern junk food is that it can cause a reward that is way more powerful than any reward the brain can get from whole foods.

Whereas eating an apple or piece of steak might cause a moderate release of dopamine, eating a Ben & Jerry's ice cream is so rewarding that it releases a larger amount.

> *"SUMMARY*
> *Eating junk food causes a release of dopamine in the brain.*
> *This reward encourages susceptible individuals to eat more*
> *unhealthy foods."*

Tolerance and withdrawal — the hallmarks of physical addiction

When a person repeatedly does something that releases dopamine in the reward system, such as smoking a cigarette or eating a Snickers bar, dopamine receptors can start to downregulate.

If the brain observes that the amount of dopamine is too high, it begins removing dopamine receptors to keep things balanced.

When there are fewer receptors, more dopamine is needed to reach the same effect, which causes people to start eating more junk food to reach the same level of reward as before. This is called tolerance.

If there are fewer dopamine receptors, the person will have very little dopamine activity and start to feel unhappy when they don't get a junk food "fix." This is called withdrawal.

Tolerance and withdrawal have been associated with addictive disorders.

Multiple studies in rats show that they can become physically addicted to junk food in the same way that they become addicted to drugs of abuse.

Of course, all of this is a drastic oversimplification, but this is basically how food addiction (and any addiction) is believed to work. This can lead to various characteristic effects on behavior and thought patterns.

> *"SUMMARY*
> *Frequent consumption of junk food may lead to dopamine*
> *tolerance. This means that a person will have to eat even more*

junk food to avoid going into withdrawal."

Cravings are a key feature of addiction

A craving is an emotional state characterized by a desire to consume a certain food. It should not be confused with simple hunger, which is different.

Cravings sometimes seem to appear out of thin air.

A person might be doing mundane things like watching a favorite TV show, walking the dog, or reading. Then suddenly a craving for something like ice cream appears.

Even though the cravings sometimes seem to come out of nowhere, they can be turned on by certain triggers, which are known as cues.

These cues can be as simple as walking past an ice cream parlor or smelling a pizza.

However, they can also be induced by certain emotional states, such as feeling depressed or lonely, a behavior known as emotional eating.

A true craving is about satisfying the brain's need for dopamine. It has nothing to with the body's need for energy or nourishment.

When a craving occurs, it can start to dominate a person's attention.

A craving makes it hard to think of something else. It also makes it hard to consider the health impacts of eating junk food.

While it isn't unusual to get cravings (most people get them in some form), repeatedly giving in to cravings and eating junk food, despite having made a decision not to, is cause for concern.

For those with food addiction, these cravings can be so powerful that they cause people to break rules they set for themselves, such as only eating unhealthy food on Saturdays.

They may repeatedly overeat, despite knowing that it's causing physical harm.

"*SUMMARY*

Regularly giving in to cravings for junk food may be a sign that someone is experiencing food addiction or emotional eating."

Cravings can sometimes turn into binges

When acting on cravings, the brain gets a reward — a feeling of pleasure associated with the release of dopamine. The reward is what cravings and food addiction are all about.

People with food addiction get their "fix" by eating a particular food until their brain has received all of the dopamine it was missing.

The more often this cycle of craving and rewarding is repeated, the stronger it becomes and the greater the quantity of food that's needed each time.

While four scoops of ice cream were enough 3 years ago, today it may take eight scoops to experience the same level of reward.

It can be almost impossible to eat in moderation when satisfying an addiction-driven craving.

That's why it's often impossible for people to just have a small slice of cake or a few M&M's. It's like telling a smoker to only smoke one-fourth of a cigarette to cut back. It simply does not work.

"*SUMMARY*
Cravings and food addiction can lead to overeating, binging, and obesity."

This can lead to complicated, addictive behaviors

Over time, food addiction can cause severe physical and psychological problems.

Many people who have been struggling with food addiction for a long time keep their eating habits a secret. They may also be living with depression or anxiety, which can contribute to addiction.

This is compounded by the fact that most people aren't aware they're experiencing food addiction. They may not realize they need help to overcome food addiction and that getting treatment for depression and anxiety can also help with addiction treatment.

"SUMMARY
People experiencing food addiction often hide their behavior from friends and family. Depression and anxiety often play a role in addictive behaviors."

Overcoming food addiction

Unfortunately, there is no easy solution to addiction. There is no supplement, mental trick, or magical remedy.

For many, it may be best to avoid trigger foods completely. Food addiction may require professional help to overcome.

Psychiatrists and psychologists can help. There are also organizations like Overeaters Anonymous (OA), which anyone can join for free.

Binge eating disorder, which is associated with food addiction, is currently classified as a feeding and eating disorder in the Diagnostic and Statistical Manual of Mental Disorders (DSM–5), the official manual that mental health professionals use to define mental disorders.

Sugar Is a "Drug" and Here's How We're Hooked

Research says that our brains are hardwired for pleasure and sugar works like many addictive drugs. So, are we sugar fiends?

Here's something to think about the next time you're craving something sweet: it could be more than just a sweet tooth. It could be an addictive itch begging to be scratched.

Brain scans have confirmed that intermittent sugar consumption affects the brain in ways similar to certain drugs.

A highly cited study in the journal Neuroscience & Biobehavioral

Reviews found that sugar—as pervasive as it is—meets the criteria for a substance of abuse and may be addictive to those who binge on it. It does this by affecting the chemistry of the limbic system, the part of the brain that's associated with emotional control.

The study found that "intermittent access to sugar can lead to behavioral and neurochemical changes that resemble the effects of a substance of abuse."

It's these findings that spurred Paul van der Velpen, head of Amsterdam's health services, to warn people that sugar is a drug, "just like alcohol and tobacco." He wrote a column on the city's public health website Tuesday calling for stronger government action regarding sugar. Actions he proposed included regulating the amount allowed in foods and also banning soft drinks in schools

"This may seem exaggerated and far-fetched, but sugar is the most dangerous drug of this time and can still be easily acquired everywhere," he wrote.

Dr. David Sack, CEO of Elements Behavioral Health, which operates Promises Treatment Centers, echoed these comments. Sack said that the prevalence and promotion of sugary foods and beverages, coupled with how it affects our brains, make addiction an issue.

"The truth is that not every one exposed to high-sugar foods is going to become addicted and seek it out regularly. The same is true with drugs like cocaine or alcohol," he told Healthline. "The difference is that we don't sell alcohol to anyone under the age of 21, but you can buy high-sugar content foods at any age.

Are We, As a Whole, Addicted to Sugar?

U.S. health officials have been less hyperbolic in their messaging than van der Velpen, but many feel equally concerned.

Earlier this year, the American Heart Association cited research that shows sugary soft drinks are responsible for 180,000 deaths worldwide each year. They recommend that adults consume no more than 450 calories per week from sugar-sweetened beverages. This translates to just under two 20-ounce bottles of Coca-Cola.

The latest numbers Trusted Source from the U.S. Centers for Disease Control (CDC) show the average American gets about 13 percent of his or her daily caloric intake from added sugars. Men, on average, get an additional 335 calories per day from added sugars, while women get about 239 extra calories per day.

While sodas are the easy culprit to blame, there are many other places where sugar sneaks into a person's diet, often without his or her knowledge.

The CDC's research shows that people consume excess sugars not only in beverages but also in foods they eat at home.

Relying on packaged or processed foods is a quick way to stack up the sugar cubes, even if they have healthy sounding names. Sugar is a common ingredient in many foods people assume are healthy.

For example, a jar of Newman's Own Tomato & Basil spaghetti sauce contains 9 grams of sugar, or about four sugar cubes. Eight ounces of V8 Fusion Vegetable & Fruit Juice contains more than 11 cubes of sugar. Yoplait Original 99% Fat Free yogurt contains between 11 and 13 sugar cubes, depending on the flavor.

How Do You Kick the Habit? Curbing Your Addiction Before It Begins

The messages telling us to crave sugar begin at an early age, Sack says. Children's TV programming is often wrapped in advertising featuring brightly colored cartoon characters selling processed foods with high sugar content.

"Food scientists have learned to manufacture food to make it more rewarding," he said. "Then they use the media, such as advertising, so they're dangling it in front of us."

Sack says that not enough parents are educating their children about healthy nutrition, and that the parents may be reinforcing bad eating habits. This is made worse when working parents are short on time to focus on meal planning.

"The biggest problem we've seen is that parents who are overweight or obese themselves feed these foods to their kids and don't see it as abnormal," he said. "Right now, parents aren't told what's appropriate nutrition for children. Unless we educate parents on what's appropriate height and weight, and what's proper nutrition, it's very hard for kids to have a proper respect for food."

Parents shouldn't stock their pantry shelves with sugary foods, should read nutrition labels on packaged foods, and should educate their children about healthy food choices, Sack said. ***"We have to recognize this is a very deep problem," he said.***

Sodapocalypse: Is There Room for Common Sense in the Soda Debate?

The debate about sugary drinks and personal freedoms should move past scare tactics to common sense solutions.

There's a can of soda in the vending machine down the hall biding its time, waiting for the perfect moment to strike.

Okay, that's probably a stretch, but soda and energy drinks are coming under heavy fire, from New York City mayor Michael Bloomberg's attempt to ban large-sized sodas to a new, cataclysmic statistic that paints soda as a serial killer.

What the debate surrounding sugary drinks lacks is reason and common sense.

180,000 Dead From Soda Each Year?

The American Heart Association (AHA) recently made waves by claiming their research shows that 180,000 deaths each year worldwide are associated with sugary soft drinks.

Researchers compared deaths from diabetes, cardiovascular disease, and cancer to the amount of soda consumed in a given country. Latin American and Caribbean countries had the most diabetes deaths—38,000—linked to the number of sugar-sweetened beverages the population consumed in 2010.

That link, however, may not be strong enough to support the

statement that sugary soft drinks are solely responsible for killing the equivalent of the population of Knoxville, Tenn. each year.

The AHA researchers demonstrated correlation, not causation. They failed to take into account numerous other factors, including a person's genetic predisposition to disease, exercise habits, stress levels, and other risk factors for diabetes, cardiovascular disease, and cancer.

There's no reason to defend soda, energy drinks, and other sugary beverages—it's not like they're good for you—but soda is being portrayed as the latest Boogeyman threatening global health, while scare tactics do little to slow the epidemic of obesity and chronic disease in Western nations.

That said, just as you shouldn't immediately accept the latest health figures without reasonable skepticism, you shouldn't blindly swallow messages from drink manufacturers either.

Athletes, Actors, and the Marketing of Sugar

Judging by the commercials, it's pretty common for someone to slam down a bottle of Mountain Dew, Red Bull, or Monster Energy before performing a stunt so huge they're transformed into a demigod. Or if they chug a Gatorade, their workout hits awe-insiring levels.

When it comes to energy drinks, you don't need extreme sports to increase your heart rate. The AHA also released a new study showing that energy drinks can create temporary irregular heart rhythms and increased blood pressure.

Their study subjects were healthy patients ages 18 to 45 who had just consumed up to three energy drinks. That's a lot—but not uncommon—for anyone to consume. A younger, healthier body can better handle the effects of a caffeine jolt, but for older patients—especially those with heart problems—the outlook isn't as bright.

"People with health concerns or those who are older might have more heart-related side effects from energy drinks," Sachin A. Shah,

Pharm.D., lead author and assistant professor at the University of the Pacific in Stockton, Calif., said in a press release.

So, if you already have a bum heart, don't "do the Dew."

Because energy drinks and soda have no known health benefits, manufacturers are feeling the heat of studies like this that link their products to health risks.

This week, Monster Beverage—the largest seller of energy drinks in the U.S.—announced it's drinks will no longer be sold as "nutritional supplements" and will instead be marketed as beverages, according to The New York Times.

The company will now have to disclose the drinks' caffeine levels—140 to 160 milligrams per 16-ounce can—but won't have to report any injuries or deaths caused by its products.

If that's a needed business strategy, think about what happens to your body when you "unleash the beast.

Your Daily Soda Intake

The AHA and other organizations aren't targeting marathoners sucking down a cup of Gatorade every few miles. Their real focus is on people who drink multiple sodas every day.

In reality, the majority of people consuming soda are far from athletes: half of Americans say they drink soda daily, and the majority (90 percent) who drink two or more glasses a day classify themselves as "somewhat overweight" or "about right," according to Gallup research. (Which, by the way, is self-reported data.)

The AHA recommends that adults consume no more than 450 calories per week from sugar-sweetened beverages, which translates to just under two 20-ounce bottles of Coca-Cola.

Cutting back on your daily soda intake will have positive health effects, but that doesn't necessarily mean that banning them in large sizes, like Bloomberg hopes to, will automatically make Americans healthier.

Yes, each soda gives you an extra eight teaspoons of sugar—on average—and those extra calories will pile up if you don't burn them off. Maybe that's why soda and energy drink advertisements often feature highly-active athletes—they're trying to burn off all that sugar.

Still, there's more to preventing diabetes and obesity than just avoiding soda. Also crucial is maintaining a healthy weight, eating a balanced diet, and staying active.

That's where common sense comes in.

The Bottom Line

Should you be guzzling down gallons of soda every day? Of course not.

Should you treat a bottle of Coca-Cola like it's a loaded weapon? No, unless of course it's diet and you're holding a pack of Mentos in the other hand.

11 Ways to Stop Cravings for Unhealthy Foods and Sugar

Food cravings are the dieter's worst enemy.

These are intense or uncontrollable desires for specific foods, stronger than normal hunger.

The types of foods that people crave are highly variable, but these are often processed junk foods that are high in sugar.

Cravings are one of the biggest reasons why people have problems losing weight and keeping it off.

Here are 11 simple ways to prevent or stop unhealthy food and sugar cravings.

1. Drink Water

Thirst is often confused with hunger or food cravings.

If you feel a sudden urge for a specific food, try drinking a large glass of water and wait a few minutes. You may find that the craving fades away, because your body was actually just thirsty.

Furthermore, drinking plenty of water may have many health benefits. In middle-aged and older people, drinking water before meals can reduce appetite and help with weight loss.

> "*SUMMARY*
> *Drinking water before meals may reduce cravings and appetite, as well as help with weight loss.*"

2. Eat More Protein

Eating more protein may reduce your appetite and keep you from overeating.

It also reduces cravings, and helps you feel full and satisfied for longer.

One study of overweight teenage girls showed that eating a high-protein breakfast reduced cravings significantly.

Another study in overweight men showed that increasing protein intake to 25% of calories reduced cravings by 60%. Additionally, the desire to snack at night was reduced by 50%.

> "*SUMMARY*
> *Increasing protein intake may reduce cravings by up to 60% and cut the desire to snack at night by 50%.*"

3. Distance Yourself From the Craving

When you feel a craving, try to distance yourself from it.

For example, you can take a brisk walk or a shower to shift your mind onto something else. A change in thought and environment may help stop the craving.

Some studies have also shown that chewing gum can help reduce appetite and cravings.

"SUMMARY
Try to distance yourself from the craving by chewing gum,
going on a walk or taking a shower."

4. Plan Your Meals

If possible, try to plan your meals for the day or upcoming week.
By already knowing what you're going to eat, you eliminate the factor of spontaneity and uncertainty.
If you don't have to think about what to eat at the following meal, you will be less tempted and less likely to experience cravings.

"SUMMARY
Planning your meals for the day or upcoming week eliminates spontaneity and uncertainty, both of which can cause cravings."

5. Avoid Getting Extremely Hungry

Hunger is one of the biggest reasons why we experience cravings.
To avoid getting extremely hungry, it may be a good idea to eat regularly and have healthy snacks close at hand.
By being prepared, and avoiding long periods of hunger, you may be able to prevent the craving from showing up at all.

"SUMMARY
Hunger is a big reason for cravings. Avoid extreme hunger by always having a healthy snack ready."

6. Fight Stress

Stress may induce food cravings and influence eating behaviors, especially for women.

Women under stress have been shown to eat significantly more calories and experience more cravings than non-stressed women.

Furthermore, stress raises your blood levels of cortisol, a hormone that can make you gain weight, especially in the belly area.

Try to minimize stress in your environment by planning ahead, meditating and generally slowing down.

> "SUMMARY
> *Being under stress may induce cravings, eating and weight gain, especially in women.*"

7. Take Spinach Extract

Spinach extract is a "new" supplement on the market, made from spinach leaves.

It helps delay fat digestion, which increases the levels of hormones that reduce appetite and hunger, such as GLP-1.

Studies show that taking 3.7–5 grams of spinach extract with a meal may reduce appetite and cravings for several hours.

One study in overweight women showed that 5 grams of spinach extract per day reduced cravings for chocolate and high-sugar foods by a whopping 87–95%.

> "SUMMARY
> *Spinach extract delays the digestion of fat and increases the levels of hormones that can reduce appetite and cravings.*"

8. Get Enough Sleep

Your appetite is largely affected by hormones that fluctuate throughout the day.

Sleep deprivation disrupts the fluctuations, and may lead to poor appetite regulation and strong cravings.

Studies support this, showing that sleep-deprived people are up to 55% more likely to become obese, compared to people who get enough sleep.

For this reason, getting good sleep may be one of the most powerful ways to prevent cravings from showing up.

> "SUMMARY
> *Sleep deprivation may disrupt normal fluctuations in appetite hormones, leading to cravings and poor appetite control.*"

9. Eat Proper Meals

Hunger and a lack of key nutrients can both cause certain cravings. Therefore, it's important to eat proper meals at mealtimes. This way, your body gets the nutrients it needs and you won't get extremely hungry right after eating.

If you find yourself in need of a snack between meals, make sure it's something healthy. Reach for whole foods, such as fruits, nuts, vegetables or seeds.

> "SUMMARY
> *Eating proper meals helps prevent hunger and cravings, while also ensuring that your body gets the nutrients it needs.*"

10. Don't Go to the Supermarket Hungry

Grocery stores are probably the worst places to be when you are hungry or have cravings.

First, they give you easy access to pretty much any food you could think of. Second, supermarkets usually place the unhealthiest foods at eye level.

The best way to prevent cravings from happening at the store is to shop only when you've recently eaten. Never — ever — go to the supermarket hungry.

> "SUMMARY
> *Eating before you go to the supermarket helps reduce the risk of unwanted cravings and impulsive buying.*"

11. Practice Mindful Eating

Mindful eating is about practicing mindfulness, a type of meditation, in relation to foods and eating.

It teaches you to develop awareness of your eating habits, emotions, hunger, cravings and physical sensations.

Mindful eating teaches you to distinguish between cravings and actual physical hunger. It helps you choose your response, instead of acting thoughtlessly or impulsively.

Eating mindfully involves being present while you eat, slowing down and chewing thoroughly. It is also important to avoid distractions, like the TV or your smartphone.

One 6-week study in binge eaters found that mindful eating reduced binge eating episodes from 4 to 1.5 per week. It also reduced the severity of each binge.

> "SUMMARY
> *Mindful eating is about learning to recognize the difference between cravings and actual hunger, helping you choose your response.*"

The bottom line

Cravings are very common. In fact, more than 50% of people experience cravings on a regular basis.

They play a major role in weight gain, food addiction and binge eating.

Being aware of your cravings and their triggers makes them much easier to avoid. It also makes it a lot easier to eat healthy and lose weight.

Following the tips on this list, such as eating more protein, planning your meals, and practicing mindfulness, may allow you to take charge next time cravings try to take over.

Healthy Eating Is Human: Joys, Challenges, and 3 Things You Can Do

If you ask a group of people what eating healthy means to them, you'll probably get a different answer every time.

For some, healthy eating means reining in a fast food habit or consuming more fruits and vegetables, while for others it may mean occasionally enjoying a piece of cake without feeling guilty.

Still yet, those who have certain medical conditions and even food allergies may conceptualize the concept of healthy eating in their own unique way.

In short, there's no single right answer to what healthy eating means.

Healthy eating is human, and as humans, we all have different wants and needs, which inevitably affect our food choices.

What's more, what healthy eating means to you may even change throughout the different stages of your life as you grow and adapt to your ever-changing needs.

This article explores the human side of healthy eating, and I provide my own go-to tips to make it easier.

What healthy eating means for me

The definition of healthy eating has changed for me a couple of times in the past few years.

By the time I was in college, healthy eating was about following nutritional guidelines and doing everything by the book. However, it meant that my view of the food on my plate had changed. I went from seeing meals I enjoyed to only seeing nutrients.

Suddenly, I went from seeing traditional rice and beans — to seeing complex carbs and plant-based proteins.

Then, when I started practicing as a nutritionist, the notion that a dietitian should look a certain way or fit into a specific body type led me to believe that healthy eating meant measuring my food to know exactly what I was consuming. I would eat whatever I wanted, as long as the nutrients I needed were accounted for.

I gave my body everything it needed to be healthy, but healthy eating goes beyond the nutrients. It's also about how it makes you feel, and with food being an essential part of culture and social events, eating should be something we enjoy.

Today I have a different approach to healthy eating. I'm far more flexible with my meals, and I understand that balance is key to being nourished and happy with food.

Healthy eating now means that, most of the time, I make sure to have food from all food groups on my plate without measuring anything or thinking about plant-based vs. animal-based protein or simple vs. complex carbs.

It also means that I get to enjoy a bit of everything — including sweets, fast food, and desserts — with moderation and without the need to measure or account for it.

As you can see, finding the balance that worked for me didn't happen overnight. On the contrary, my definition of healthy eating has been changing as I've gone through the different stages of my life.

As long as you aim to nourish your body and listen to what it needs, you can also give healthy eating your own meaning, because healthy eating is for everyone.

"SUMMARY
For me, healthy eating is about nourishing your body and being at peace with food at the same time. Your definition of healthy eating may change over time as you mature and your priorities change."

Seeing the bigger picture

As with many things in life, eating healthy doesn't always end up as you planned.

You may find yourself stuck at work late at night or too tired to prepare a home-cooked dinner, and that doesn't mean that you shouldn't order take-out and actually enjoy it.

If healthy eating means being flexible with what you eat, you'll need to learn to adapt to the circumstances, which may happen more often than not.

In cases when I'm choosing food on the spur of the moment, I try to opt for the best choice out of what I'm given. Whenever I can, I try to order the closest thing to a home-cooked meal or go for a sandwich, salad, or bowl.

Yet, sometimes I do crave some pizza — so I eat and enjoy that, too!

At times like this, I remember to see the bigger picture. That is, that healthy eating is not defined by single meals but by the choices we make day after day.

A close friend once told me a saying that goes, "One bad meal will not make you sick, just as one good meal will not make you healthy."

"SUMMARY
When it comes to eating healthy, one meal doesn't define your habits — your overall food choices do."

It may be challenging sometimes

When you're a dietitian, many people think that eating healthy comes naturally to you. Yet, we're human beings, too, and we love dessert and crave foods like anybody else.

In my case, one of the biggest challenges I've had to face was when I had to give up most carb-containing foods to manage recurring infections.

Carbs are present in many food groups, including grains, starchy vegetables, legumes, fruit, and dairy. They're also present in processed foods and sweets.

Experts often categorize them into two groups according to their fiber content:

Whole grains: retain their naturally occurring fiber

Refined carbs: are processed to remove their fiber and contain added sugar

In theory, I was supposed to eliminate refined carbs, which some people would argue is the healthiest thing to do.

However, in practice, I ended up giving up all kinds of processed carbs, including whole wheat bread and pasta, alongside starchy vegetables, grains, and dairy.

Thus, the list of carb-rich foods I could eat was limited to fruits, oats, quinoa, and legumes — lentils, beans, chickpeas, and edamame.

Some people told me that this transition wouldn't be so hard for me as a dietitian. However, it took me a while to adjust to my new eating pattern, especially when planning on-the-go snacks or eating out.

I learned that organization and creativity are key to managing my nutritional needs.

"*SUMMARY*
Regardless of the reason, changing eating habits is challenging for everybody."

The bottom line

We're all humans who are constantly growing and adapting to change, and so does our concept of healthy eating.

Here I shared with you how the definition of healthy eating has changed for me through the years, the biggest challenge in my healthy eating journey, and my tips and tricks to make healthy eating easier.

However, my way definitely isn't the "right way" — or the only way — to eat healthy. It's only what works for me, and it may or may not work for you.

Healthy eating is human, and it looks different for each and every one of us. Consider what you could do in your own routine to set yourself up for success with healthy eating.

If you're unsure about where to start, consider working with a registered dietitian, as they can help you conceptualize a sustainable, nutritious eating plan that works for your specific needs and lifestyle.

6 Foods That Keep You Awake at Night

Getting enough restful sleep is essential for overall health.

In fact, chronic sleep deprivation can affect both your physical and mental well-being and increase your risk of certain health conditions, like heart disease and type 2 diabetes.

Many factors, including your food choices, may make it harder for you to fall and stay asleep.

Foods and beverages that may keep you awake at night.

1. Caffeinated foods and beverages

When you think of foods and drinks that give you immediate energy, coffee and other caffeinated products may come to mind.

This is because caffeine is a central nervous system stimulant, meaning it increases feelings of alertness and makes you feel more awake and energized.

Because of this effect, caffeinated foods and beverages, including soda, coffee, caffeinated tea, and caffeinated chocolate products may negatively affect sleep and keep you awake at night.

In fact, research shows that consuming coffee, even many hours before bedtime, can affect sleep. A small 2013 study in 12 people found that consuming 400 mg of caffeine at bedtime, as well as 3 and 6 hours before bed, significantly disrupted sleep.

Interestingly, ingesting 400 mg of caffeine 6 hours before bed more than doubled the time it took for participants to fall asleep and reduced total sleep time by 1 hour, compared with a placebo.

This lack of sleep due to caffeine consumption may lead you to drink a lot of caffeine the next day to counteract feelings of tiredness, which can negatively affect the next night's sleep. Some people refer to this cycle as the coffee cycle.

While some people are very sensitive to caffeine and experience sleep-related issues even if they consume a small amount, others can have caffeinated beverages closer to bedtime without experiencing sleep issues. This is due to genetic variations.

So, even though experts recommend cutting back on caffeine to promote restful sleep, it's especially important if you're sensitive to caffeine.

Foods that contain caffeine include:
- chocolate
- coffee, including decaf, though in lower amounts than regular
- foods that contain kola nut as an ingredient
- green and black teas
- guarana
- yerba mate
- energy drinks
- foods that contain caffeine or coffee as an ingredient, such as tiramisu

What if you want to stay awake?

If you're using caffeine to stay awake, say for a night shift, it might not be the best plan. Studies show that using caffeine to stay awake for night shifts and to shift sleep to the following day may lead to significantly decreased sleep quality overall.

In a 2006 study in 34 people, half of the participants followed a standard sleep routine of sleeping at night, while the other half stayed up at night and slept during the day. Both groups ingested 200 mg of caffeine before bedtime.

Both groups experienced sleep disturbances, including difficulty falling asleep, compared with those who took a placebo.

However, caffeine more negatively affected the participants who slept during the day. Only this group experienced decreased sleep duration and decreased deep REM sleep after consuming caffeine.

A 2018 study in nighttime shift workers found that those who consumed more caffeine had greater sleep disturbances and psychological distress.

Thus, even though caffeine may give you a temporary boost of energy, it may keep you from getting restful sleep.

> "*SUMMARY*
> *Caffeine is a central nervous system stimulant and may negatively affect sleep, especially if you consume it within 6 hours of bedtime. It may give you a temporary boost of energy, but ultimately have a negative impact on sleep duration and quality.*"

2. Spicy foods

Eating spicy foods close to bedtime may keep you awake for several reasons.

Spicy foods are known to cause indigestion and worsen symptoms of heartburn and acid reflux.

When you lie down to go to sleep, these spicy food-related symptoms can become worse, as acid may travel into the esophagus, causing irritation. This can keep you awake at night and lead to sleep disturbances.

Therefore, if you experience heartburn after eating spicy foods or you have acid reflux, you may want to steer clear of spicy foods before bed.

Eating very spicy foods, like chili peppers, slightly increases your core and surface body temperature.

This effect is temporary. However, some researchers have proposed that an increase in body temperature from eating spicy foods before bed may negatively affect sleep. Elevated body temperature is linked to sleep disturbance.

> "*SUMMARY*
> *Spicy foods may lead to indigestion and reflux symptoms, which may disturb your sleep. Eating spicy foods before bed may lead you to feel warm, which can negatively affect sleep.*"

3. High glycemic index foods and added sugar

Foods that have a high glycemic index (GI) rapidly increase blood sugar levels. These foods include refined carbs like white bread, sweets, and foods with high amounts of added sugars.

That said, research on the effects of high GI foods on sleep shows mixed results. Some studies link high GI diets with insomnia and sleeping issues, while others suggest a high GI meal decreases the amount of time it takes people to fall asleep.

A 2019 study that included data on more than 77,000 women found that those who followed a high glycemic diet were more likely to have insomnia over a 3-year follow-up period.

The study also found that consuming added sugar and refined carbs was associated with higher odds of insomnia.

Other studies have shown that diets high in sweets, sugar-sweetened beverages, and refined carbs were associated with poor sleep quality.

A 2016 study that included data on 18,779 adults found that people who slept 5 hours per night or less had a 21% higher intake of sugar-sweetened caffeinated beverages, compared with those who slept 7 hours per night or more.

It's important to note that this study was observational. So, it only shows there was an association, but it can't say for certain what caused people to lose sleep.

In addition, the people in this study may have slept less due to the caffeine in the beverages, not just the sugar.

There are several reasons why a high glycemic diet and foods high in added sugar and refined grains seem to be associated with poor quality sleep.

High GI foods cause significant spikes and drops in blood sugar levels. This triggers your body to release hormones, like adrenaline, cortisol, and growth hormone, which can lead to symptoms like anxiety, hunger, and irritability.

Studies show that low blood sugar may reduce sleep efficiency. On the other hand, high blood sugar after a high glycemic meal may initially make you feel sleepy, but the resulting changes in hormones, including insulin, may cause you to wake up later in the night.

High glycemic diets also trigger inflammatory responses in the body and create imbalances in beneficial intestinal bacteria, which may also affect sleep.

"*SUMMARY*

High glycemic diets and diets rich in added sugars may negatively affect sleep. Consuming foods high in added sugar close to bedtime may lead to insomnia and difficulty staying asleep."

4. Fatty foods

Eating foods high in fat, like fried chicken and fatty meats, may contribute to poor sleep.

Research shows that greater fat intake, especially saturated fat, may negatively affect your sleep pattern.

A 2016 study in 26 adults found that a higher intake of saturated fat was associated with lighter, less restorative sleep.

Another study that included 459 women found that the more total fat and saturated fat participants consumed, the lower their total sleep time.

A 2015 study in 211 men demonstrated that men who had insomnia had a higher intake of saturated fat than men who didn't have sleep disorders.

Additionally, a 2016 study that analyzed data on 15,273 men found that men with insomnia had diets higher in trans fats than men without insomnia.

Additionally, having a heavy, fatty meal later at night may affect your ability to fall asleep.

This may be because your digestive tract slows when you're sleeping, so eating a fatty meal may overwhelm the digestive system, leading to discomfort that can keep you awake at night.

Furthermore, high fat foods are known to exacerbate symptoms of acid reflux, which may keep you awake at night.

"*SUMMARY*
Diets high in total, saturated, and trans fats may lead to sleep disturbances and keep you awake at night."

5. Fast food and other ultra-processed foods

Ultra-processed foods like fast food and packaged snacks may not be the best choice for restful sleep.

Research consistently links diets high in ultra-processed foods to poor sleep quality and short sleep duration.

A 2018 study that included data on 118,462 adolescents aged 12–18 discovered that shorter sleep duration and poor sleep quality was associated with higher intakes of fast food, instant noodles, and sweets.

A 2020 study investigating the sleep habits of Brazilian adolescents linked poor sleep quality to a higher intake of ultra-processed foods. No available studies looked at the effects of ultra-processed foods on sleep in adults specifically.

The results of the 2020 study aren't surprising, considering the nutritional composition of ultra-processed foods. These foods tend to be high in ingredients linked to sleep disturbances, including refined carbs, added sugar, and saturated and trans fats.

What's more, diets high in ultra-processed foods can lead to weight gain. Studies show that people with overweight or obesity tend to have more sleep issues than people without

Obesity may lead to obstructive sleep apnea, a health condition that can make it hard to breathe at night, resulting in sleep loss.

"*SUMMARY*
Studies have found links between ultra-processed foods and poor sleep quality. Cutting back on ultra-processed foods is beneficial for overall health and may help you get a better night's sleep."

6. Alcoholic drinks

Many people like to have a drink or two at night to relax and unwind before bedtime. In fact, alcohol is one of the most commonly used sleep aids.

Even though having a few drinks may initially make you feel tired, studies show that drinking can cause sleep disturbances and keep you awake at night.

Interestingly, alcohol causes you to fall asleep faster, but then significantly disrupts sleep during the night as your blood alcohol levels decline.

A 2020 study in 11,905 people found that higher alcohol consumption was significantly linked to poorer sleep and shorter sleep duration.

A 2019 study in 25 people found that consuming a large amount of alcohol significantly reduced total sleeping time and self-reported sleep quality.

Because alcohol is so strongly linked to insomnia, healthcare professionals usually recommend avoiding alcohol before bed as part of insomnia treatment.

If you regularly drink alcohol before bed to relax or as a way to fall asleep, it's important to understand that, although alcohol will likely make you tired at first, it will negatively affect your overall sleep quality and may keep you awake later in the night.

"*SUMMARY*
Alcohol reduces the time it takes to fall asleep, but it leads to sleep disturbances later in the night. To promote restful sleep, it's best to avoid drinking alcohol before bed."

The bottom line

If you have difficulty falling or staying asleep, avoiding certain foods and beverages may help.

Studies have linked caffeinated foods and beverages, added sugar, refined carbs, spicy foods, high fat foods, and alcohol to poor sleep quality and shorter sleep duration.

To promote restful sleep and minimize the chances of waking up at night, consider limiting or avoiding the foods and beverages on this list, especially later in the day and before bedtime.

We have to treat food addiction as we would any other life-threatening addiction—we have to resist addictive foods with every fiber of our being

and recommit to that fight on a daily, hourly, minute-to-minute basis. Vigilance is imperative to the recovery process

so stay healthy..............

THIRTEEN

IDENTIFYING MOLLY

Molly, or MDMA, can come in a pill, capsule, powder, or crystal form. This drug is illegal in the United States and can have serious risks. MDMA (3,4-methylenedioxy-methamphetamine) has a reputation as a party and club drug. It's known for boosting mood, energy, compassion, and sensory perception, as well as for its hallucinogenic effects.

Generally, MDMA is taken in capsules, although it also comes in liquid or powder forms. Also called "molly," MDMA is illegal and unregulated in the United States. This makes it very difficult to know what you're getting when you purchase or take molly, and that can be dangerous.

"

The name "molly" is short for "molecular." Molly is used as a slang term for 3,4-methylenedioxy-methamphetamine (MDMA). Sometimes it specifically refers to the powder form of MDMA, but it's often used as slang for any type of MDMA. The name "molly" comes from the way the drug is bought and consumed. It's thought to be a pure "crystalline" or "molecular" powder form of MDMA by people who use it."

The many forms of molly

There are several forms of MDMA. It's common for people to refer to MDMA by alternate names, such as "molly" or "ecstasy."
People most often take molly as a tablet or capsule. However, people sometimes take molly as a liquid or powder. The powder form can be snorted or swallowed.

"*The crystal form of MDMA looks similar to rough quartz crystal.*"

What does pure molly look like?

"Pure molly" is a way to refer to the powder form of MDMA. Since there are no regulations, its exact look can vary. However, in most cases, pure molly is white or yellow and looks similar to sugar.

What does molly look like in pill form?

The pill form of molly can take on several appearances. Pills and capsules often resemble prescription or over-the-counter medications. They can come in a variety of shapes and colors. Often, pills are imprinted with a logo. These logos are usually simple symbols, such as a clover, smiley face, or checkmark.

"*IN ANY FORM, MOLLY IS ILLEGAL IN THE U.S.*
MDMA is listed as a Schedule I substance. This classification is used for substances that have a high potential for addiction and misuse.

However, this may change in the future. Some studies are finding therapeutic uses for MDMA in treating certain mental health conditions, like post-traumatic stress disorder (PTSD)."

is molly safe to use?

There are several risks associated with molly. One of the largest is that it's impossible to tell how much MDMA you're getting with any pill, capsule, liquid, or powder. You might end up with a much larger or much smaller amount than expected.

Additionally, many molly pills and powders are mixed with other substances. These can include:

ketamine

heroin

methamphetamine

cocaine

caffeine

cough medicine

synthetic cathinones ("bath salts")

Contamination can increase the chances of a bad reaction or unpleasant effects. It can also lead to dangerous drug interactions that are difficult to predict.

Since it's unlikely you'll know exactly what substance was mixed into the molly you consumed, you won't know what caused your negative experience.

A negative experience with molly can cause effects like:

nausea

heart palpitations

teeth clenching

muscle tension

insomnia

blurry vision

sweating

chills

dehydration

Long-term effects of molly

There are other risks associated with the long-term use of molly. As is the case with most psychoactive drugs, molly can affect the way

your brain produces important chemicals.

Molly enhances the activity of the neurotransmitters norepinephrine, dopamine, and serotonin. In turn, this can increase your heart rate, energy, and mood, respectively. But this increased activity also causes a depletion in your brain's naturally produced chemicals.

Over time, molly use can deplete the amount of serotonin in your brain. This can lead to depression and anxiety.

Additional long-term effects of molly depend on the person and the amount of molly used but might include:

> *addiction*
> *memory problems*
> *lack of focus*
> *frequent colds*
> *liver damage*
> *kidney damage*

FOURTEEN

ARE YOU SHOPAHOLIC (SHOPPING ADDICTION)

Whether it's the latest gadget, a chic new piece of clothing, or even food, we've all felt the urge to splurge now and again. This comes as little surprise because we are constantly bombarded with online, print, and media ads that reinforce shopping mentality. Indulging in occasional spending isn't necessarily a bad thing when it done in moderation and doesn't disrupt family finances.

If your urge to shop becomes uncontrollable and if you are constantly spending beyond your means on things that you don't need, a shopping addiction can be just as damaging as gambling or alcoholism. Fortunately, there are ways to break free from shopping addiction. If you have tried to quit spending with little or no luck, you may need the help of friends, family, or a supportive treatment program to kick the compulsion to shop.

Shopping addiction, also known as compulsive buying disorder, or compulsive shopping, affects about 18 million adults in the United States. It's described as the compulsion to spend money, regardless of need or financial means. While many people enjoy shopping as a treat or as a recreational activity, compulsive shopping is a mental health disorder and can cause severe consequences.

The American Psychiatric Association (APA) does not officially recognize shopping addiction as a distinct disorder, and considerable debate surrounds the legitimacy of the disorder.

People with this disorder may be addicted to a certain product, such as clothes or jewelry, or may also buy anything from food and beauty products, to stocks or real estate.

The person with a shopping addiction gets the same rush or high from making purchases as someone who misuses drugs gets from using. Once the brain associates shopping with this pleasure or high, the person with a shopping addiction will try to recreate it again and again.

Little is known about this addiction. ResearchTrusted Source is mixed, with some studies showing that women are more likely to have this addiction than men. Other research has shown that men and women have an equal risk of developing the disorder.

Some studies show that the average age of a person with a shopping addiction is 30. Other studies show that it happens between ages 18 and 20, when people are able to establish their own credit. However, more research still needs to be done.

The Cycle of Shopping Addiction

People who struggle with compulsive shopping may experience ups and downs in their addiction. The urge to shop is usually strongest during moments of depression, sadness, or anger. Shopping addiction has also been associated with holidays that reinforce compulsive shopping, i.e. holiday shopping in December.

People who struggle with a shopping problem initially feel a "high" or "rush" from the act of shopping. However, any positive feelings they get from gratifying their compulsion are fleeting.

"Many people feel deep regret, shame, or embarrassment in the aftermath of a shopping spree, which ultimately leads to more feelings of distress and more shopping."

Some people contain their shopping problem to online shopping. Sprees on sites like Amazon.com can also play into problem shopping patterns, and are often just as devastating as in-person shopping. The ability to quietly and quickly buy more through online merchants can lead to shopping sprees in the middle of the night, during work breaks, or from the comfort of the living room sofa. These sprees are often extremely financially devastating and can be hard to control.

Compulsive shopping often follows a distinct pattern:

Anticipation. This includes ruminating on possible shopping trips or items

Preparation for shopping. This may include making lists, compulsively looking online, researching items, or talking about shopping.

Shopping. The act of shopping can take place in person or online. This includes adding items to online shopping carts or physically picking items up in the store.

Spending. Spending is the final act when a financial transaction is made and the items are given to the shopper.

Problems Associated with Compulsive Shopping

People with shopping addiction often spend beyond their means. Although it may appear less harmful than other forms of addiction, such as drug or alcohol abuse, shopping addiction can and does create serious problems. Financial problems are the most obvious problems associated with compulsive shopping.

Without anything to stop the issue, people with this issue often spend until they absolutely can no longer buy new things. This may mean they have run out of money, maxed out their credit cards, and are unable to borrow funds to continue to feed the addiction.

Shopping addiction may cause financial and even legal problems if those who suffer are unable to fulfill their other financial obligations because of their addiction.

People with compulsive shopping disorder may resort to borrowing money from family and friends in order to fuel their addiction. Relationships with loved ones may grow strained over time because people with shopping addiction have a tendency to continually borrow even if they lack the capacity to pay back their debt.

> *"The shame and desire to hide spending often strains marriages and relationships. This can lead to strained or broken relationships because even patient and loving partners eventually become unable to cope with the consequences of the addiction."*

In some cases, compulsive shopping impacts the person's credit score, which may prevent him or her from buying a home or a reliable vehicle. In some cases, low credit scores may impact the ability to be hired for a job. Severe cases of shopping addiction may also lower a person's ability to work, and online shopping during work hours may lead to job termination.

Left unresolved, compulsive shopping can become just as problematic and self-destructive as almost any other form of addiction.

Shopping Addiction: What Causes It?

There's not a single known cause of shopping addiction, but there may be several contributing factors.

While the developers of the DSM-5 have chosen not to include shopping addiction, the 2014 review notes that some of the symptoms of craving and withdrawal some people experience could be similar to other addictions. "Shopping can act as a distraction from unpleasant emotions," explains Schiff. She adds that addiction involves both physical and psychological factors. Physically, the brain chemicals released during shopping can give people a "high," she explains, while psychologically, people may shop for things to help them cope with stress or feel a sense of control.

Stress and anxiety are the most significant underlying causes of shopping addiction," adds Sehat. Many people turn to gratifying behaviors as coping mechanisms, she says. "The endorphins released make the individual feel happy and less stressed."

The aforementioned 2021 statement from the APA suggested that there's evidence that social isolation and stress may increase the risk of developing a shopping addiction. These dynamics could have been at play while many people spent more time at home, carrying extra stressors, and in isolation during the COVID-19 pandemic — and could have plausibly caused an increase in these types of behaviors. The authors of the paper noted, however, that this is just a theory, and currently there's no hard evidence to say one way or the other that this happened.

Certain environmental risk factors have also been found to put people at a higher risk of developing shopping addiction. For example, having a higher income or having credit cards may make compulsive buying more accessible. Changes in your personal environment, such as a divorce, or moving away from your loved ones, could also influence emotionally driven compulsive buying, as some people report shopping to alleviate feelings of loneliness, helplessness, or guilt.

The 2012 review has also suggested that shopping addiction may coincide with mental health conditions involving impulsivity and compulsiveness, including obsessive-compulsive disorder (OCD), personality disorders, anxiety disorders, and binge-eating disorder. It may also be linked with affective disorders, such as depression. Other research noted that shopping addiction tends to run in families, particularly families living with mood, anxiety, or substance use disorders.

But having any of the above mental health conditions doesn't mean you will automatically develop a shopping addiction, and vice-versa

Addicted to shopping 7 Signs You May Have A Problem

Shopping addiction is easy to hide, thanks to online buying. Here's how to tell if your shopping habit is a sign of a serious problem.

A 2016 meta-analysis suggests that about 4.9 percent of Americans are addicted to shopping. The prevalence is even higher among university students (8.3 percent) and among shoppers (16.2 percent).

The advent of Internet shopping makes it easier to buy in the comfort and privacy of your own home, potentially increasing the rate of shopping addiction. You don't have to spend thousands of dollars or go into debt to be addicted to shopping--although these are certainly red flags.

Here are some signs you might have a problem.

1.Negative Emotions and Low Self-Esteem

Shopping can be a distraction from unpleasant emotions, offering a temporary high that may help people feel better about themselves or less anxious. A 2014 analysis highlights a number of emotional risk factors for shopping addiction, including:

·low self-esteem

·low self-regulation (the ability to control your behavior and act in your own best interests)

·negative emotions

·cognitive overload (feeling like one has few brain resources)

You are especially likely to be a shopping addict if you use shopping to manage negative emotions.

2.Preoccupation With Shopping

Planning your expenditures is a good way to manage your budget. But if you find yourself spending significant time thinking about shopping, you may have a problem. Some examples of shopping preoccupation include:

·spending significant parts of the day shopping or planning purchases

·thinking about shopping when you should be doing something else

·being distracted from conversations by thoughts of shopping

3.Shopping in Secret

It is easier than ever before to shop in secret, thanks to online buying. People with shopping addictions may shop in secret to conceal their purchases or because they feel guilty about their behavior.

4.Being Unable to Stop Shopping

People with a shopping addiction feel unable to stop shopping. They may resolve to quit and successfully do so for a while, then return to shopping. Stress can trigger this relapse. So too can denial that there is a problem. Because we live in a society that requires everyone to shop, it's easy to dismiss problem shopping as normal. Relapsing compulsive shoppers may gradually increase their spending such that it does not feel as harmful as it is.

5.Compromising Your Values or Well-Being to Shop

One of the hallmarks of addiction is that it causes a person to indulge in the addiction even when doing so is harmful. People with a shopping addiction may make choices they regret to shop, or even do things that endanger themselves or others. Some examples include:

·spending more than you can afford

·avoiding paying bills to shop

·taking on more debt than you can manage

·taking money from other people to shop

compromising your values to shop, such as by using money you intended to give to charity to buy things

6.Feeling Guilty About Purchases

Most people buy things they don't need every now and again. Some may even feel guilty about these purchases. Chronic guilt about shopping, however, may signal a problem--especially if a person continues to shop in spite of this guilt.

7.Needing to Shop to Feel Normal

For people without a shopping addiction, buying something can be a fun diversion or a necessity. People with compulsive buying disorder feel compelled to spend money so that they can feel normal. When you can't shop, you might feel angry, frustrated, or grumpy. You might feel like you will be unable to enjoy your life if you cannot shop. The frustration of being unable to shop is a common reason people who are trying to quit relapse.

Emotional Symptoms of a Shopping Addiction

Like all addicts, shopping addicts may try to hide their addiction, and if a loved one is addicted to shopping, they may try to hide it from you. If you hide credit card bills, shopping bags or receipts, you may be a shopaholic. In some cases, shopaholics may try to hide their addiction by lying about just one element of it. For instance, a person may admit they went shopping, but they may lie about how much they spent.

Some of the other emotional symptoms you may notice from a shopaholic include the following:

·Spending more than they can afford

·Shopping as a reaction to feeling angry or depressed

·Shopping as a way to feel less guilty about a previous shopping spree

·Harming relationships due to spending or shopping too much
·Losing control of the shopping behavior

Physical Symptoms of a Shopping Addiction

Although most addictions have physical symptoms related to them, shopping addictions may not. In most cases, the symptoms you experience due to your shopping addiction will be emotional in nature. The physical evidence of a shopping addiction may include a declining financial situation.

Short-Term and Long-Term Effects of a Shopping Addiction

The short-term effects of a shopping addiction may feel positive. In many cases, you may feel happy after completing a shopping trip. However, these feelings are often mixed with anxiety or guilt, and in most cases, the guilt or anxiety may propel you back to the store for even more shopping.

The long-term effects of a shopping addiction can vary in intensity and scope. Many shopping addicts face financial problems, and they may become overwhelmed with debt. In some cases, they may simply max out their credit cards, but in other cases, they may take out a second mortgage on their home or charge purchases to their business credit card. If you are addicted to shopping, your personal relationships may also suffer. You may end up getting a divorce or distancing yourself from your parents, children or other loved ones.

Is There a Test or Self-Assessment I Can Do?

If you are still trying to figure out whether or not you are a shopaholic, Shopaholics Anonymous suggests that you ask yourself the following questions. If you answer "yes" to many of these questions, you may have an addiction. The questions are:
·Do you shop when you feel angry or disappointed?

·Has overspending created problems in your life?

·Do you have conflicts with loved ones about your need to shop?

·While shopping, do you feel euphoric rushes or anxiety?

·After shopping, do you feel like you have just finished doing something wild or dangerous?

·After shopping, do you ever feel guilty or embarrassed about what you have done?

·Do you frequently buy things that you never end up using or wearing?

·Do you think about money almost all the time?

Medication: Are There Shopping Addiction Drug Options?

Unfortunately, according to MSN Money, the research on drugs that may treat shopping addictions has not revealed any conclusive evidence about which sort of drugs may be the most helpful in treating this issue. However, many shopaholics have been able to successfully treat their addictions by turning to anti-anxiety medications or even antidepressant medications.

Shopping Addict Drugs: Possible Options

Reviewing an article from the Annals of Clinical Psychiatry, ABC News reports that a drug called memantine may be able to help shopaholics. Designed to treat Alzheimer's, this drug may be able to help shopaholics make decisions more clearly, and it may also help them to avoid compulsive behavior.

Medication Side Effects

The side effects of these drugs vary depending upon which medication you decide to use. If you decide to take antidepressants, for instance, you may experience any of the following side effects:

·Nausea

I·nability to fall asleep at night
·Feelings of anxiousness
·Unexplained sweating
·Feeling tired or fatigued a lot
·Headaches

Ideally, you should speak with your doctor about possible side effects before you start taking any medication.

Drug Addiction, Dependence and Withdrawal in Shopaholics

Withdrawal symptoms may vary from person to person, but according to the Chicago Tribune, many shopping addicts will experience withdrawal symptoms that are similar to the withdrawal symptoms experienced by people who are addicted to drugs or alcohol. If you feel irritable, depressed or out of control after shopping, you may be experiencing withdrawal, and you may need to get help.

Depression and Shopping

According to Donald Black from the University of Iowa, as quoted in Esperanza magazine, nearly two-thirds of all shopaholics struggle with depression or anxiety. In order to effectively treat your shopping addiction, you may also need to deal with your other mental health issues. Ideally, when searching for a recovery program, you should try to find a recovery program that can address both aspects of your addiction.

Dual Diagnosis: Substance Abuse and Shopping

In some cases, shopping addictions can be related to a substance abuse issue. If you believe that you are, or a loved one is, struggling with substance abuse and a shopping addiction, it is time to get help. With the right professional shopping addiction treatment, you will be able to gain control over your life again.

Shopping addiction treatments

Family therapy — Because addictions don't only affect one person, you may want to enroll in family therapy to help combat a shopping addiction you or someone you know is dealing with. This helps with accountability and responsibility for actions. For example, you may be encouraged to share receipts or bank statements with a spouse or loved one to encourage honesty and limit unnecessary spending.

Cognitive behavioral therapy — In this type of psychotherapy you address unhealthy or negative behaviors that may contribute to compulsive buying disorder. Through a number of discussions with a mental health worker, you will be able to not only address these behaviors but also understand how to view them and respond in a more positive and productive manner.

Treatment of comorbidities — As with many addictions, the presence of comorbidities (two or more chronic diseases or conditions) may exist. Excessive shoppers may be battling with depression and anxiety or other mental disorders and use compulsive buying as a means to feel better about themselves. Addressing these comorbidities can also lead to combatting your shopping addiction.

Financial counseling — Because people who suffer from shopping addiction spend compulsively regardless of potential consequence — debt, no finances, stealing — some sort of financial counseling can help benefit them in the long run. Not only will they see the results of their actions, but groups like Debtors Anonymous can provide a communal support system of others going through similar situations.

Getting Help for a Shopping Addiction

"It isn't fun to feel out of control or depressed about shopping too much. It isn't pleasant to lose those close to you due to the arguments that may occur as a result of your shopping addiction. If you are, or a loved one is, struggling with a shopping addiction, it is time to get help now."

FIFTEEN

GAMBLING ADDICTION

For many people gambling is an enjoyable activity without becoming a problem, but over time, some individuals develop a gambling addiction. This can ruin their lives.

Gambling addiction is like other addictions. It is a progressive illness – it can evolve into a huge problem sooner or later. It is also obsessive and compulsive. The urge can be overwhelming. The gambler will do anything – lie, cheat, and con, manipulate, blow up savings – to indulge in gambling.

Usually, there are several signs or symptoms when normal recreational gambling progresses into a problem. The earlier the signs are recognized and problem identified, the better the chances of successful recovery.

Problem gambling is hard to recover from, but possible with professional help.

Understanding Gambling

A gambling compulsion can actually start the first time someone places a bet, and it can gradually progress into an addiction over time. According to experts, how long it takes for someone to develop a problem varies by the individual, though compulsions tend develop more quickly in people who engage in continuous forms of gambling, such as online betting. Some gamblers exhibit symptoms of a compulsion in less than a year, while with some it may progress slower.

When does gambling become a problem?

Most people who bet don't have a gambling problem, but some people become compulsive gamblers at some point in their life. People in this group lose control of their betting to the point that it negatively impacts their life.

Pathological (harmful) gambling can be a form of addiction. People with a gambling addiction can't control their urge to gamble, even if they are losing a lot of money. They are willing to risk something of value in the hope that the reward will be more valuable. Gambling addiction can seriously affect all areas of life. Consequences of problem gambling can include financial losses, bankruptcy, losing a job, homelessness, mental health conditions and the breakdown of personal relationships. They can be serious not only for you, but also for members of your family and for your friends and associates. If you are caring for someone with an addiction, it is important that you also continue to look after yourself.

symptoms of gambling addiction

People with addictions often try to hide their condition, but a gambling addiction can be difficult to conceal. You may need frequent access to casinos or online gambling pools. Even if you gamble at home when no one is around, your addiction may begin to show itself in other areas of your life.

If you have a gambling addiction, you may display some or all of the following behaviors:
- obsessing over any type of gambling
- gambling to feel better about life
- failing to control your gambling

•avoiding work or other commitments to gamble
•neglecting bills and expenses and using the money for gambling
•selling possessions to gamble
•stealing money to gamble
•lying about your gambling habit
•feeling guilty after a gambling session
•taking bigger and bigger risks while gambling

You may also experience the following consequences from your gambling addiction:
•disintegrating relationships or friendships
•loss of house, job, car, or other personal possessions

People with gambling addiction don't always gamble frequently. But when they do start gambling, they may be unable to stop.

Does someone I know have a gambling addiction?

People with gambling disorder often hide their behaviour, but there are warning signs that gambling has become a problem for someone you know.

People with gambling problems may struggle with financial difficulties. Signs of financial troubles you may notice include:
•borrowing money regularly
•having multiple loans
•unpaid bills
•lack of food and household essentials
•missing money or household valuables

Addiction can also cause changes in a person's mental health and wellbeing. Signs of these changes you may notice include:
•conflict with others
•unexplained absences from important events or commitments
•poor performance at work or school, and/or taking more sick days
•feelings of helplessness, depression or feeling suicidal
•withdrawing from family or at work
•changes in personality or mood

·an increase in alcohol or drug use

Do I have a gambling addiction?

If you have a gambling addiction, you are likely to experience some of the following:

·spending more time and money on gambling than you intend to

·'chasing' losses: gambling to win back what has been lost, particularly after heavy losses

·constant thoughts about gambling, and feelings of irritability or restlessness if you try to stop gambling

·resorting to gambling as a way of coping with a bad mood, anxiety or depression, or feelings of helplessness or guilt

·lying to cover up the extent of your gambling

·missing important things in your life because of gambling, including family events, work or appointments

·relying on others for financial support after heavy gambling losses

What causes gambling addiction?

When you have a gambling addiction, an area of your brain called the insula may be overactive. This hyperactive region may lead to distorted thinking. This can cause you to see patterns in random sequences and continue gambling after near misses.

Your brain may respond to the act of gambling in the same way that an alcoholic's brain responds to a drink. The more you feed your habit, the worse it will become.

Why do people keep gambling?

Many factors may increase a person's chances of developing problems with gambling. Sometimes, people turn to gambling to escape from other difficulties in their lives.

Society accepts gambling and sees it as a part of normal life. That makes it very hard for people with a problem to keep away from it. Gambling is a form of addiction. People with a gambling problem can have similar chemical changes in their brains to those seen in people addicted to alcohol or drugs.

Where can I get help with gambling addiction?

Certain types of psychological therapy, for example cognitive behaviour therapy (CBT), may help someone overcome gambling addiction. Cognitive behaviour therapy involves looking at the logic behind gambling, such as the odds of winning, beliefs about luck and skill in non-skills-based games, and the likelihood of 'chasing' your way back to financial security.

Psychological therapies can also address underlying problems such as anxiety, depression or social isolation.

Some gamblers may find financial counselling helpful in offering alternatives to gambling as a way to **financial recovery**.

If you think that you or someone you know may have a gambling addiction, speak to your doctor. If needed, your doctor can provide a referral to a **psychologist.**

How is gambling addiction treated?

With the right treatment, gambling addiction is manageable. Unlike someone with a food addiction, you don't need the object of your addiction to survive. You simply need to learn how to develop a healthy and balanced relationship with money.

It's important for you to quit gambling completely, since even occasional gambling can lead to a relapse. A program of recovery can help you develop impulse control. In general, gambling addiction is treated with similar methods as other addictions.

Inpatient rehabilitation program

Although not frequently required, some people find that they need the structure afforded by an inpatient program at a treatment center to overcome a gambling addiction. This type of program may be especially helpful if you're unable to avoid casinos or other gambling venues without help. You will need to stay in the treatment facility for a set amount of time, anywhere from 30 days to an entire year.

Outpatient rehabilitation program

Outpatient treatment programs are more commonly used by people with gambling addictions. In this type of program, you will attend classes at a facility. You may also attend group sessions and one-on-one therapy. You will continue to live at home and participate in school, work, or other daily activities.

Psychotherapy or cognitive behavioral therapy

In addition to group counseling or support sessions, you may also benefit from one-on-one therapy. Gambling addiction can stem from deeper emotional or avoidance issues. You will need to deal with these underlying issues in order to change self-destructive patterns, including your gambling addiction. Counseling gives you a place to open up and address these problems.

Medication

In some cases, you may need medication to help you overcome your gambling urges. Your gambling addiction might result from an underlying mental health condition, such as bipolar disorder. In these cases, you must learn to manage the underlying condition to develop better impulse control.

Lifestyle changes

Dealing with the financial consequences of gambling is sometimes the hardest part of the recovery process. In the beginning, you may need to turn over financial responsibilities to a spouse or trusted friend. You may also need to avoid places and situations that can trigger your urge to gamble, such as casinos or sporting events.

What is the outlook for gambling addiction?

Like any addiction, compulsive gambling can be difficult to stop. You may find it embarrassing to admit that you have a problem, especially since many people gamble socially without developing an addiction. Overcoming the shame or embarrassment that you feel will be a big step on the road to recovery.

A recovery program, one-on-one counseling, medication, and lifestyle changes may help you overcome your gambling addiction. If you don't treat your gambling problem, it can lead to serious financial issues. It can also negatively affect your relationships with family members, friends, and others. Effective treatment can help you avoid these consequences and mend your relationships through recovery.

> *"Gambling can be just as addictive as drugs and Alcohal. Teens and their parents need to know that they are not just gambling with money they are gambling with their lives"*
> ...

SIXTEEN

IS VIDEO GAME ADDICTION REAL ?

It's great to do things you enjoy. But can you go too far with a hobby? And at what point does it become an addiction? That's the question experts are trying to answer about playing video games.

Even though gaming has been around for almost 50 years, studies about its harms are still in the early stages. Different groups have come to different conclusions about whether problem playing should be called an addiction.

The World Health Organization added "gaming disorder" to the 2018 version of its medical reference book, International Classification of Diseases. But the American Psychiatry Association's manual, the(**DSM-5)** didn't. (So far, gambling is the only "activity" listed as a possible addiction.)

Video game addiction, also called internet gaming disorder, is a condition characterized by severely reduced control over gaming habits, resulting in negative consequences in many aspects of your life, including self-care, relationships, school and work.

This condition can include gaming on the internet or any electronic device, but most people who develop significant gaming issues mainly play on the internet.

Whether internet and video gaming addiction should be classified as an addiction or mental illness is debated among researchers.

Many researchers consider video game addiction a behavioral addiction similar to gambling disorder, in which the rush of winning becomes one of the main reasons for playing.

Others think this comparison to gambling is flawed because there may not be financial or material losses involved with playing video games. In addition, winning a video game may require cognitive skills and sharp reflexes, while winning at gambling is mainly a matter of chance.

Regardless of this debate, any activity or habit that becomes all-consuming and negatively impacts your daily functioning can cause significant mental, social and physical health issues. It's important to seek medical care if you think your video game habits are taking over your life.

Who does video game addiction affect?

Video game addiction can affect children, teens and adults, although adults are most likely to have this condition. People assigned male at birth are more likely to have video game addiction than people assigned female at birth.

How common is video game addiction?

Researchers estimate that video game addiction affects between 1.7% and 10% of the U.S. population. The estimated range is large because many researchers disagree on the diagnostic criteria for internet gaming disorder.

What are the signs and symptoms of video game addiction?

Signs and symptoms of video game addiction (internet gaming disorder) include:

·Poor performance at school, work or household responsibilities as a result of excessive video game playing.

·Withdrawal symptoms, such as sadness, anxiety or irritability, when games are taken away or gaming isn't possible.

·A need to spend more and more time playing video games to get the same level of enjoyment.

·Giving up other previously enjoyed activities and/or social relationships due to gaming.

·Being unable to reduce playing time and having unsuccessful attempts to quit gaming despite the negative consequences it's causing.

·Lying to family members or others about the amount of time spent playing video games.

·A decline in personal hygiene or grooming due to excessive video gaming.

·Using video games as a way to escape stressful situations at work or school or to avoid conflicts at home.

·Using video games to relieve negative moods, such as guilt or hopelessness.

If you or a loved one are experiencing these signs and symptoms, talk to your healthcare provider or a mental health professional.

What causes video game addiction?

Researchers are still trying to determine the exact cause of video game addiction and the addictive qualities of internet and video games.

So far, researchers think the process of playing and winning video games may trigger a release of dopamine. Dopamine is a brain chemical (neurotransmitter) that plays a key role in several bodily functions, including pleasurable reward and motivation. Dopamine is the same neurotransmitter involved in other use disorders, including gambling disorder and substance use disorder.

Recent neurological research shows similarities in the brains of people with video game addiction and substance use disorders.

How is video game addiction diagnosed?

To be diagnosed with video game addiction (internet gaming disorder), your healthcare provider may refer you to a mental health professional such as a psychologist or psychiatrist.

Mental health professionals use the American Psychiatric Association's Diagnostic and Statistical Manual of Mental Disorders (DSM-5) to diagnose mental disorders, which includes information about internet gaming disorder.

Your mental health professional will ask questions about your medical and personal history, including gaming patterns and more. In general, for internet gaming disorder to be diagnosed, your gaming behavior patterns must be extreme enough to result in significant impairment to your personal, family, social, educational and/or occupational functioning. These patterns usually have to exist for at least one year.

How is video game addiction treated?

The main treatment option for video game addiction (internet gaming disorder) is talk therapy (psychotherapy).

Psychotherapy is a term for a variety of treatment techniques that aim to help you identify and change troubling emotions, thoughts and behaviors. Working with a mental health professional (such as a psychologist or psychiatrist) can provide support, education and guidance to you and your family.

Specific types of psychotherapy that may benefit someone with video game addiction include:

Cognitive-behavioral therapy (CBT): This is a structured, goal-oriented type of therapy. A therapist or psychologist helps you take a close look at your thoughts and emotions. You'll come to understand how your thoughts affect your actions. Through CBT for video game addiction, you can unlearn negative and obsessive thoughts and behaviors and learn to adopt healthier thinking patterns and habits.

Group therapy: This is a type of psychotherapy in which a group of people meets to describe and discuss their problems together under the supervision of a therapist or psychologist. Group therapy is a valuable source of motivation and moral support for people who have video game addiction, especially if they've lost contact with friends or peers as a result of their video game addiction.

Family or marriage counseling: This type of therapy can help educate loved ones about the disorder and create a more stable home environment.

If you have another underlying mental health condition, such as depression, anxiety or attention-deficit/hyperactivity disorder (ADHD), your healthcare provider may recommend certain medications to treat the symptoms of the condition....

What are the risk factors for developing video game addiction?

Researchers are still learning about video game addiction (internet gaming disorder). So far, they've established some factors that may put people at higher risk for developing the condition.

Psychological risk factors related to internet gaming disorder include:

- Impulsivity.
- Low self-control.
- Anxiety.

Behavioral risk factors related to internet gaming disorder include:

- Spending an increasing amount of money on gaming.
- Increasing weekday gaming time.
- Attending offline gaming community meetings.
- Having a gaming community membership.

Should all people who play video games or online games be concerned about developing an addiction to

them?

Studies show that video game addiction affects only a small number of people who play online games or video games.
If you play video games, it's important to be aware of the amount of time you're spending playing them. This is especially important if you're starting to neglect other daily activities, such as hygiene, social interactions and school and/or work. These behaviors could be early signs of video game addiction.

When should I see my healthcare provider about video game addiction?

If you're concerned for yourself or a loved one about possible video game addiction and related problems, talk to your healthcare provider or a mental health professional.
If you've been diagnosed with video game addiction, it's important to seek treatment and to stay committed to your treatment plan. You'll likely need to see your mental health provider regularly.

Millions of people across the world play video games and internet games. While the majority of people who enjoy these types of games don't develop problematic behaviors, it's possible for gaming to become all-consuming and negatively impact your daily functioning. If you're worried about your gaming habits or those of a loved one, reach out to your healthcare provider. They're always available to help you.

SEVENTEEN

HOW YOUR ENVIRONMENT AFFECTS ADDICTION

Whether you love an addict or you are one, confronting an addiction to substances like drugs or alcohol is scary. When you discover that someone is addicted to drugs or alcohol, it's completely natural to want to find out what "caused" their addiction. After all, many people believe that understanding what causes addiction can help to "fix" it. While there is some truth to this — rehab is designed to address the factors that led to addiction — it's not always easy to identify the cause of addiction on your own.

Why?

Because addiction is typically the combination of several factors — genetic, environmental, and social. And, while many addicts share similar stories, their spiral into addiction is a unique path that wound around many of their own individual circumstances. This can make it difficult to know how to support and understand your loved one, not only as they seek treatment initially, but also in the days and weeks that follow their formal treatment.

You see, just because someone completes their formal rehab program does not mean they are done being an addict. The real work of overcoming an addiction is done when the individual begins to rebuild their life outside of a treatment facility. It takes hard work, dedication, and intense effort to reconcile old hurts and move forward into new jobs, new relationships, and a new way of viewing the world.

Genetics and Environment: Which Causes Addiction?

There has long been a debate about whether addiction is caused by a person's genetic makeup or the environment they inhabit. Researchers believe genetics can influence a person's predisposition toward addiction to substances once they begin using them. In other words, some people may have a gene or genetic component that predisposes them to addictive behaviors if they are introduced to certain substances.

Environment, which is defined as family beliefs and attitudes, peer group, community, and more, is also believed to heavily influence addiction because these are typically the factors that lead an individual to try drugs or alcohol initially. When a person is encouraged to try drugs or alcohol, either socially or as a coping mechanism, they may continue to use these substances and, over time, their use may spiral into addiction.

Truthfully, most doctors and researchers agree that addiction is the result of a combination of genetics and environment. One does not necessarily outweigh another, and both should be a significant consideration when determining the best course of treatment for an addict. For example, if a person's father was addicted to alcohol, there may be something in their genetic makeup that will also lead them to become an alcoholic if they begin drinking.

While it is important to understand the hereditary component of addiction, knowing the environmental causes of addiction and the way the environment can influence addiction and recovery is essential. Why? Because if you do not understand the impact that an addict's environment has on their ability to get clean, you are not setting them up for success after they complete their formal rehab and treatment program.

Environmental Risk Factors for Addiction

As we mentioned before, environmental risk factors are the things and people that an addict is surrounded by on a regular basis. Typically, they fall into one of six categories:

1. Family

Not only does the type of family a person grew up in have a big impact on the likelihood that they will become an addict, but it also will have a huge impact on their ability to recover from addiction and pull their life back together. For example, if an individual grew up in a home with a lot of conflicts or without an adult they could look up to, they may be more disposed toward addiction. Individuals who grew up in a home where alcohol or drug use was prevalent are also at higher risk of becoming addicted later on.

2. School

A student's performance in school, their commitment to their education, and the availability of quality friendships can be a factor in addiction. This is true for adolescents, teens, and even young adults who may be facing the college party scene. If an individual is older, their work environment may play a big role, especially if they are employed in a high-stress, high-stakes job and are in need of a release from all of the pressure.

3. Peers

A person whose friends engage in drug use and abuse is far more likely to do the same. In fact, more than any other factor, this is considered the biggest risk factor for addiction. However, it's not just close friends that can influence a person's use of drugs or alcohol. It could be an extended peer group at school or the general attitude of the school's student body when it comes to drugs or alcohol. Or, on the opposite end of the spectrum, a person who is bullied or not included in any of their school's peer groups may seek solace in drugs or alcohol to cope with their loneliness.
Media also can play a big role in influencing this kind of behavior, particularly in adolescents and teens who watch actors on TV or in movies engaging in these kinds of behaviors. Unfortunately, drugs and alcohol are often glorified in the media, being used and joked about in ways that seem fun and easy and don't always show the consequences of their use.

4. Community

If a person lives in a community where drug use — and abuse — is prevalent, they will be more likely to fall into it themselves.

5. Trauma

There is a proven link between sexual abuse and adult addiction to drugs or alcohol, particularly if the abuse occurred during a person's childhood. While this has some connection with our earlier mention of the link between family environment and addiction, it is important to understand trauma as its own entity because of the increased risks associated with individuals who have experienced sexual abuse.

6. Mental Illness

Addiction can also be a byproduct of mental illness, especially anxiety and depression. People who suffer from a mental illness may find that using drugs or alcohol to "self-medicate" makes them feel better. Sometimes they may not know they have a mental illness — they may just know that having a few drinks before a party helps them calm down. But, eventually, this can spiral out of control because someone who is using alcohol or drugs in this manner will gradually need to use more and more to achieve the same "high" they experienced in the beginning.

Creating a Sober Living Environment

It can be hard to look back and realize that some of the factors listed above led someone you love down the road of addiction. However, it's not too late to make some changes to encourage health and healing. Just as a person's environment can create risk factors for addiction, it can also play an instrumental role in helping an addict work through recovery and successfully get their addiction under control.

A professional rehabilitation program — even the best ones out there — cannot follow an addict out into the "real" world. Once an addict successfully completes a formal rehab program, it's time for them to re-learn how to function under "normal" living conditions. So what does this mean?

It means they will have to learn how to cope with things that may have contributed to their stress — and ultimately addiction — in the past. They may have to reassimilate into their family or find a job or cope with past trauma. A lot of this work will continue through counseling and outpatient therapy. However, there are also certain things recovering addicts and their loved ones can do to encourage a sober living environment.

1. Create a Low-Stress Environment

This will look different for every addict in recovery, so it's important to talk with your loved one about what they need. If you are the recovering addict, then it's essential you speak up and make your needs known. Don't be afraid to distance yourself from negative influences, such as friends who engage in drug and alcohol use, or a family member who abused you as a child. At the same time, don't be afraid to ask for help. Maybe it's time to stop living alone and move in with a trusted family member or friend who can provide support and accountability during recovery.

Wherever you choose to live, it's vital that the home environment be low-stress and not mimic the environmental triggers that contributed to your slide into abuse initially. If you are inviting a loved one to live with you while they continue their recovery journey, take time to make your home bright and welcoming, providing them with a light, positive atmosphere that makes them feel comfortable and supported.

2. Avoid Major Triggers

Just because a person completes a rehab program does not mean that they are "cured." While it may not always be the case, setbacks and relapses can happen. But, the best way to support a recovering addict is to make sure their home environment is free from triggers that could encourage them to relapse. They need to learn how to trust people again, and this will happen when they are in an environment where they are cared for. The best way to do this is to provide them with a drug and alcohol-free environment to help them continue to fight and overcome the urges their addiction causes.

If you are a recovering addict, surround yourself with people who will encourage your successes, not people who will tempt you to fall back into your old patterns. This may mean leaving your old roommates and finding a new home. It may mean avoiding places you used to go to a party and drink. Decide what you need and make sure to express those needs to your support system.

3. Don't Try to Do It Alone

Whether you are a recovering addict or you are supporting one, it's going to be difficult to navigate this journey if you don't have the support you need. No matter what your experiences have been, you have likely felt a lot of anger and hurt as addiction has wrapped itself around you and your family. It will take time to sort out all of the feelings and experiences that stemmed from addiction and learn how to move forward.

For some, it can take the form of professional counseling. For others, it may be an addiction support group. And this is not just for a recovering addict — family and friends of addicts should take advantage of the resources available to them as well. Whether you are a listening ear or you have taken on a larger role of accountability or caretaking, you need someone you can talk to and process things with.

You Can Do It Believe In Yoursef

Stop your addiction Focus on something which is very important like school, college or university focus on your health and diet, build good relation with valuable people like parents and siblings And lastly ask forgiveness from your ♡Lord♡ and ask him to help you stay on right path because your ♡Lord♡ will forgive you but your nervous system never

☆So be patient and never giveup☆